Social work with Gypsy, Roma and Traveller children

Daniel Allen and Paul Adams

Published by
British Association for Adoption & Fostering
(BAAF)
Saffron House
6-10 Kirby Street
London EC1N 8TS
www.baaf.org.uk

Charity registration 275689 (England and Wales) and SC039337 (Scotland)

© Daniel Allen and BAAF, 2013

British Library Cataloguing in Publication Data
A catalogue record for this book is available from the British Library

ISBN 978 1 907585 78 4

Project management by Jo Francis, Publications, BAAF
Designed and typeset by Helen Joubert Design
Printed in Great Britain by the Lavenham Press

BAAF is the leading UK-wide membership organisation for all those concerned with adoption, fostering and child care issues.

Contents

1	**Introduction**	**1**
2	**Gypsy, Roma and Traveller communities**	**4**
	The different communities	5
	Population size	9
	History of oppression	10
3	**Social policy context**	**14**
	Accommodation	14
	Education	17
	Health	18
	Social work	19
	Criminal justice	20
	Invisibility	20
4	**Ethnicity, cultures, traditions and beliefs**	**22**
	Nomadism	22
	Ethnicity	23
	Pride in family and community	24
	Religion	25
	Cleanliness and hygiene	25
	Animals and livestock	26
	Gender roles and sexuality	26
	Privacy and attitudes to authority	28
5	**The law and social work with children**	**30**
	The legal context	30
	Implications for children in care	33
	Legal summary	37
	Social work in practice: mistrust and non-engagement	38
	Numbers of children in care	40

6 Experiences of the care system   **43**

On the edge of care   43

Coming into care   45

Feeling different: racism and abuse   48

Relationship with family and community   51

Secrecy and stigma   52

7 Anti-discriminatory casework   **54**

Engaging Gypsy, Roma and Traveller families   54

A children's rights approach   60

8 Promoting cultural competence   **66**

Racial awareness   67

Multicultural planning   69

Contact   71

Survival skills   72

Training for cultural competence   73

9 Placement issues   **75**

Family and friends care   75

Assessment and support   76

Fostering   78

Adoption and permanence   85

Leaving care   88

10 Conclusions   **90**

Themes   90

Recommendations for policy makers   91

Recommendations for local authorities   91

Recommendations for fostering and adoption services   92

Recommendations for practitioners   92

Useful organisations   **94**

Bibliography   **97**

Acknowledgements

We are grateful to the people who helped develop the idea for this good practice guide and who sat on the Gypsy and Traveller Social Work Working Group: Sarah Cemlyn, Annie Lau, Yvonne McNamara, and John Simmonds. We are particularly grateful to Sarah for her detailed and expert consideration of our first draft.

Thanks also go to Alexandra Plumtree and Sarah Coldrick for their legal advice, and we very much appreciated the involvement of Sarah Bevan, Lynrose Kirby, Keith Miller and Eilis Milson who all read and commented on the first draft. We are also very grateful for the contributions from Chantelle Gray, Sue (foster carer), Carol (respite foster carer), Alison, Jill Parker and Gaba Smolinska-Poffley.

Shaila Shah, Jo Francis and the BAAF Publications Team have offered helpful advice and turned a manuscript into the finished article. We thank everyone mentioned for their time and encouragement, and acknowledge that the limitations of the final text rest entirely with the authors.

This guide has been kindly supported by funding from the Esmée Fairbairn Foundation.

Note

For reasons of confidentiality, names have been changed in a number of case studies and quotes within this book.

The authors of this good practice guide recognise that there has been limited work in this area, that this text is a starting point, and that there is much more work to be done. We welcome and encourage contact from social workers, foster carers, adopters and Gypsy, Roma or Traveller people who may have comments, observations or experiences to share in relation to this work. Please do not hesitate to contact either Daniel Allen at Allend@edgehill.ac.uk, or Paul Adams at paul.adams@baaf.org.uk.

Note about the authors

Daniel Allen is a senior social work lecturer at Edge Hill University, and has been working with Gypsy, Roma and Traveller young people, families and communities for 11 years. Starting his career as a residential childcare support worker in 2002, Daniel worked with a number of Irish Traveller children. Over five years, he developed a critical insight into some of the challenges that Irish Traveller families can face when accessing and making sense of social work and other public services. In 2007, Daniel moved into a Disabled Children's Team. Here, he was able to engage Irish Traveller and Romani Gypsy young people and their families, to assess, plan, implement and evaluate tailored packages of support.

In 2009, Daniel secured funding from the Economic Social Research Council to complete a Masters in Social Work Research and a PhD. These two programmes of study enabled him to consolidate his knowledge and understanding of social work with Gypsy, Roma and Traveller groups. The title of Daniel's PhD, *Changing Relationships with the Self and Others: An interpretative phenomenological analysis of a Traveller and Gypsy life in public care*, can be accessed via the De Montfort University Open Research Archive (DORA). Whilst completing this period of study, Daniel also spent some time working as a child protection social worker in the North of England. This unique experience provided him with the opportunity to develop a key understanding of some of the challenges being faced by Roma young people in particular.

The development of this Good Practice Guide represents a culmination of these experiences. Daniel's other works include a chapter on the failings of social policy with Gypsy and Traveller communities. This can be found in Richardson J and Ryder A (eds) *Gypsies and Travellers: Accommodation, empowerment and inclusion in British society*, published by Policy Press. In addition to developing research in this area, Daniel continues to support social work practice with Gypsy, Roma and Traveller communities in the North West of England where he lives and works.

Paul Adams qualified as a social worker in 1993, having been inspired by working as a foster carer in the US. His background is predominantly in local authority children's services, managing child care and fostering teams.

Paul joined BAAF as a Fostering Development Consultant in 2010, and additionally chairs fostering and adoption panels, and provides consultancy and training. He has recently authored two guides for BAAF: *Parent and Child Fostering* (with Elaine Dibben, 2011) and *Planning for Contact in Permanent Placements* (2012).

He lives in North Wales with his partner Sarah, and rescue dogs Simba and Bluebell.

1

Introduction

Discrimination against Gypsies and Travellers appears to be the last "respectable" form of racism. It is still considered acceptable to put up "No Traveller" signs in pubs and shops and to make blatantly prejudiced remarks about Gypsies and Travellers.

(Trevor Phillips, former Chair of the Commission
for Racial Equality, 2004)

This is the context in which this good practice guide has been developed; it aims to assist social workers, foster carers, and others working with Gypsy, Roma and Traveller children who are subjects of social work interventions, including those who are living in care. It is written from a perspective that recognises the need for better practice if Gypsy, Roma and Traveller children are going to be well supported to live safely with their birth families, and, where children do need to enter care, to grow up with a strong sense of pride in their cultural identity and heritage.

This good practice guide is structured in the following way:
Chapter 1 serves to introduce the issues, and **Chapter 2** describes the various individual groups and communities who come together under the wider terms of "Gypsy", "Roma" and "Traveller". **Chapter 3** looks at the social policy context, focusing on accommodation, education, health, social work and criminal justice matters. **Chapter 4** discusses the cultures, traditions and beliefs of Gypsy, Roma and Traveller people to the extent that it is possible without making stereotypes about these matters, and **Chapter 5** sets out the legal framework in the UK for working with Gypsy, Roma and Traveller children and families, and considers what that means in practice.

In some ways, the chapters that make up the first half of the guide constitute a detailed background of what needs to be understood before moving on to the more specific aspects of what it means to work with Gypsy, Roma and Traveller children in a social work context. **Chapter 6** then summarises the work by Allen (2013), who explored the experiences of Gypsies and Travellers who lived in care as children, and **Chapter 7** sets out the need for an anti-discriminatory approach to casework, looking at engaging with Gypsy, Roma and Traveller families, children's rights, advocacy and empowerment. **Chapter 8** offers a framework that promotes the development of cultural competence in working with or looking after Gypsy, Roma and Traveller children, and **Chapter 9** discusses issues in family and friends care, fostering, adoption and leaving care. **Chapter 10** brings together the various themes in a conclusion with recommendations, and useful organisations are listed at the end of the guide.

Before setting out, it is important to recognise that there are some very obvious limitations to this good practice guide. The idea of writing something that deals with, and actively includes all Gypsy, Roma and Traveller groups in the same short publication is challenging because such attempts to generalise always carry a risk of stereotyping. It is nevertheless felt to be better to risk this than to exclude specific groups, particularly as experience of discrimination and oppression is likely to be much the same across all the Gypsy, Roma and Traveller communities. For this reason, the principles of good practice with Gypsy, Roma and Traveller children and families are widely applicable.

It is also the case that any "culture" will be hard to accurately describe, consisting as these groups do of many different families and individuals. One option to address this difficulty would be to avoid descriptions of group culture and history entirely, but this would have produced a guide that was so vague as to be of little value to the reader. With this in mind, however, it is important to be careful about how this guide is used, always remembering that individual children and families are the experts on themselves, their culture, and their own situations.

It needs to be acknowledged that research in this subject area is limited. With the notable exceptions of Cemlyn (2000a; 2000b; 2006; 2008) Garrett (2002; 2004a; 2004b; 2005) Morran (2001; 2002) and Power (2004), there has been little discussion about these issues in social work arenas. Neither has there been much effort to seek community perspectives in a structured and meaningful way, leaving a fairly blank canvas on which to set out the issues.

This guide is written to recognise the context of discrimination and oppression experienced by Gypsy, Roma and Traveller communities. It is written from a perspective that recognises the current weaknesses of social care (and other state provision) in relation to Gypsy, Roma and Traveller families, and in particular acknowledges that the needs of Gypsy, Roma and Traveller children are not well met in the care system. Whilst these concerns are set out, it important to note that this guide does not blame social workers and others for poor practice. It is recognised that social work takes place in a complex societal structure, and that this structure determines the context and organisation of social work practice. However, neither is it suggested that social workers should be complacent, and the guide clearly suggests that practitioners and others need to better understand Gypsy, Roma and Traveller cultures, mores and traditions. On this basis, it sets out what is required to achieve an anti-discriminatory approach within a culturally competent framework of care.

Where possible, the guide attempts to offer a positive way forward, at the same time acknowledging societal realities. At times there is clear direction about what constitutes good practice; at other times, the text sets out the challenges and dilemmas that need to be considered within the context of practice generally, and in meeting the needs of an individual, family, group or community. Engaging with the issues is a first step in better understanding how to work effectively with Gypsy, Roma and Traveller communities and how to better parent and care for children from Gypsy, Roma and Traveller backgrounds. The challenge that follows this is to improve the outcomes for all Gypsy, Roma and Traveller children.

2

Gypsy, Roma and Traveller communities

There is an inherent danger of stereotyping when trying to describe any group of people, and this is certainly the case for Gypsy, Roma and Traveller communities. As with any discussion on culture, identity, social, historical, and political representation, understanding the positions of Gypsy, Roma and Traveller children, families, groups and communities is complicated because of the challenges in defining both the particular and the general. This means that social workers need to exercise caution in how they use broad descriptions of communities, being careful to understand that families and individuals are all different, and have their own identities and perspectives. In working with people, it is their own situation, and how they experience that, which is the most important aspect, and this concern must never be lost to wider generalisations.

In a concerted effort to avoid generalisation, the brief descriptions that follow should not be seen as a means to achieve a comprehensive understanding of the unique nature of Gypsy, Roma and Traveller communities. Instead, it is hoped that they show that each group included under these terms has a very distinct culture which has endured to survive centuries of persecution and oppression.

As shown through the many examples pertaining to the marginalisation, oppression and subjugation of minoritised groups, the social representation of "people" is often shaped by historical perception. This social view is crucially important when considering the way in which the stereotypical perspective of Gypsy, Roma and Traveller communities has emerged from a general ignorance, or projected racism within the population at large. Frequently represented in unhelpful and inaccurate media as being "socially deviant" (Richardson, 2006), Gypsy, Roma and Traveller communities in the UK have themselves been subject to extreme forms of violence, hostility and social marginalisation since the 16th century. This historical experience and representation is not only responsible for the continued marginalisation of these communities, but also a dominant view which often misrepresents the Gypsy, Roma and Traveller way of life.

It is not always well recognised that the groups of people who are frequently referred to as "Gypsies" or "Travellers" actually constitute a rich and diverse group of communities which each go under different names, and often distinguish themselves sharply from one another. While the following brief descriptions may be considered simplistic by community members and other specialists, those practitioners new to this area of social work should find them helpful in beginning to develop an important understanding of specificity and to establish the necessary foundations from which to build cultural competence in this area.

THE DIFFERENT COMMUNITIES

Groups included and associated with the terms "Gypsy", "Roma" and "Traveller"

Romani (English) Gypsies

Romani Gypsies, Romanichal, or Romani chals as they are sometimes termed, often speak Romani, or *pogadi chib*, which has its origin in an ancient Sanskrit language that was first spoken in the Indus Valley, in the northwestern region of the Indian subcontinent, over a thousand years ago. It is thought that Romani Gypsies originally came to Europe from India some time in the 13th or 14th century; they were first recorded in British history in 1502, and have maintained a distinctive culture since this time. Despite recent developments in equality legislation, Romani Gypsies continue to fight for cultural survival, including facing eviction, criminalisation and racism in the context of acute and systematic social exclusion (Cemlyn *et al*, 2009).

The word "Gypsy"

The word "Gypsy" in English and "Gitanos" in Spanish is not a Romani word but a distorted version of the word "Egyptian". The word "Gypsy" is often used by non-Gypsies to identify, or label, the whole Travelling population, and is frequently used within the media and by other non-Gypsies as a racist term of abuse, especially when abbreviated. Many Travelling people are content to use the term Gypsy to describe themselves, unless they are in the company of settled people, where, because of the negative imagery associated with the word, they may reject the term. This is particularly relevant for some Roma communities, since in Sinti, a variation on the Romani language, the English word "Gypsy" literally translates as "dirty".

Roma

Roma populations across Europe are members of the same ethno-social group as Romani Gypsies. However, rather than coming to the UK in the 16th century, their ancestors settled in other European countries (mainly in Central and Eastern Europe) earlier in the migration process. Although Roma families have been arriving in the UK for centuries, their migration has been driven in recent times by their experiences of poverty and racism in their home countries. Cook *et al* (2010) point out that Roma families report the desire to come to the UK in search of greater economic and social justice, and yet many Roma in the UK work for low wages on temporary contracts. The report also shows that most Roma in the UK live in sub-standard accommodation, shared with other families, leading to poor health and low school attendance by children. Drawing on the research findings of European Dialogue (2009) and Poole and Adamson (2008), Ryder and Greenfields (2010) report how the barriers and restrictions on employment, particularly on people from Romania and Bulgaria, add further disadvantage to this group.

Irish Travellers

Another principal Traveller group in the UK is the Irish Travellers, sometimes self-referred to as "Pavees" within the Irish Traveller community. Although some of their traditions may be similar to those of Romani Gypsies, McVeigh (1997) states that Irish Travellers have their origins in a Celtic, and possibly pre-Celtic, nomadic population in Ireland. According to Niner (2002), they have travelled within the UK since the 19th century, but the inclusion of the words "counterfeit Egyptians" in the 1562 Punishment of Vagabonds Calling Themselves Egyptians Act, suggests that Irish Travellers might have been in the UK well before that date.

Irish Travellers have shared the discriminatory experiences of Gypsies, with waves of legislation that have had a significant and adverse effect on their way of life, cultural survival and economic well-being.

Scottish Gypsies/Travellers

Families choosing to identify themselves as Scottish Gypsies or Travellers vary geographically. Some families with strong Highland connections tend to regard themselves as Travellers, whereas families from the Lowland and Border areas often regard themselves as Gypsies. Historic records also indicate that Scottish Gypsy/Traveller families may sometimes call themselves Nawkens or Nachins.

Some of these families have connections with Romani Gypsy and Romanichal families. Travelling metalworkers were recorded in Scotland as early as the 12th century.

Welsh Gypsies

Welsh Gypsies have similar origins to Romani Gypsies. Their history positions them as being descendants of Abram Woods, a celebrated violinist reputed by Welsh Gypsies to be the first person to introduce the violin into Wales, and other families who migrated in the 17th and 18th centuries from the South West of England to Wales. Welsh Gypsies have been nomadic for many years, as shown by court records and Welsh literature, which first recorded them as a distinct group in 1579. It is now believed that many Welsh Gypsies came from Spain via France and landed in Cornwall, subsequently making their way to Wales (Jarman and Jarman, 1998). For generations, they have lived their nomadic lives separate from the Welsh community. Although today they mostly live in houses, they have tended to retain their distinct customs and traditions.

The importance of self-definition

When working with Gypsy, Roma and Traveller children, families, groups and communities, it is important to enable them to decide whether they self-define as "Gypsy", "Roma", "Traveller", or prefer some other term. While some individuals may associate with the term the professional chooses, others may not, and respecting the preferred identity and name of each group is an important aspect of culturally competent practice. It avoids assumptions, and is the first step towards developing cultural understanding.

New Travellers

The term "New Traveller" is used to describe a community that lives as Travellers but who are not generally from a Romani Gypsy, Irish Traveller, Scottish Gypsy/Traveller or Welsh Gypsy background. While the word "New" denotes a community of people originating mainly from the settled UK population (Earle et al, 1994), not all New Travellers would use this term and may simply refer to themselves as "Travellers" or "vehicle-dwellers". Others might avoid the term "Traveller" altogether, due to negative or confusing anti-Traveller stereotypes (Hetherington, 2000).

Martin (2002) explains that people in the UK have taken to the road for centuries, often as a reaction to social and economic pressures. The present-day "New Traveller" movement originated from people seeking an alternative way of life in the early 1970s, but it should be noted that some are second- and third-generation New Travellers. New Travellers often struggle to receive acknowledgement of their distinct culture, identity and values within UK society, and although the history of this group may be different from older and more established Gypsy, Roma and Traveller groups, their experiences of inequality and marginalisation are very similar.

Showmen and Circus People

Showmen and Circus People are defined as being members of 'a distinct organised group of "travelling showpeople"' (Department for Communities and Local Government, 2007, p 8). They generally live, move and work across the country providing entertainment, and although their heritage can be traced back through recorded history, the lack of basic public services continues to marginalise them and disenfranchise their position in society as a distinct social and occupational group.

Although the economy of Showmen and Circus People is based on selling entertainment to the public, the refusal of some local authorities to allow circuses often has grave consequences for children and families (Power, 2007). While being a distinct group within the wider Gypsy and Traveller community, Showmen and Circus People are not legally recognised as a specific ethnic group and are not therefore protected by the wider frameworks of race equality legislation.

Boat People

Boat people, or "Bargees", as some prefer to be known, are a group of Travellers who have historically lived and worked on barges throughout the UK's canal system. The first canal to be built in England was the St Helens canal which opened in 1757, and by the early 19th century canals connected industrial towns across England and Wales. Currently, there are relatively few families still working on the network of inland waterways, although many narrow boats have been converted into living accommodation and families are choosing to live and travel on the canals and rivers.

The challenges experienced by Boat People relate to economic pressures and inaccurate definition. For those individuals and families who might travel the rivers and canal networks for occupational reasons, the lack of policy guidance regarding the definitions of "home mooring" and "continuous cruising" represents a continued threat to their cultural mores and economic sustainability. The National Bargee Travellers Association therefore believes that additional and specific measures are needed to protect boat dwellers from harassment, unlawful eviction, boat repossession and homelessness (Environment, Food and Rural Affairs Committee, 2012).

POPULATION SIZE

Historically, Gypsies, Roma, and Travellers were not included in any formal National Census because they were not recognised by government, despite being part of British society for over 500 years. The 2011 Census enabled Gypsies, Roma and Travellers, for the first time, to volunteer their ethnicity and it was reported that 57,680 people living in England and Wales have chosen to do so. However, these figures contradict the Commission for Racial Equality (2006) which gives a national approximation of between 270,000 and 360,000 Gypsies, Roma and Travellers living in the UK.

Since 2003, the Government has been able to obtain and publish national figures about the number of Gypsy, Roma and Traveller children in schools. It should be noted that these figures apply to Travellers of Irish Heritage and Gypsy/Roma pupils, while Ofsted reports include a broader range of children, including Fairground and Circus families, New Travellers, bargees and others living on boats. In terms of numbers in 2012, the Department for Education reports that there were 3,350 Travellers of Irish heritage and 10,335 Roma/Gypsy children enrolled in schools. This increased monitoring has revealed the extent of educational inequality. Statistics have shown that Gypsy and Traveller pupils remain disadvantaged in the education system in comparison to other minority ethnic groups. They are the group most at risk of leaving school without any qualifications, and are less likely than other groups to make the transition to secondary school (Ofsted, 1999).

Despite the positive move to include Gypsy and Traveller children in the various census data sets, the format for doing this falls short of what is actually required. The terms used for their ethnic compartmentalisation – "Gypsy/Roma" or "Traveller of Irish heritage" – are problematic. The clear inadequacy presented in both of these returns is in the failure to include Romani Gypsies, Roma, Scottish Gypsies/Travellers, Welsh Gypsies, Showmen and Circus People, Boat People and New Travellers, all of whom are distinct groups within the UK. This means that the numbers who make up the wider Gypsy, Roma and Traveller community remain unknown. Furthermore, failing to distinguish the term "Gypsy and Roma" means that we cannot know accurate numbers for either group because their own sense of identity and separateness from one another is not represented. In response to a parliamentary question on 19 December 2012, Don Foster, the Parliamentary Under Secretary of State for the Department for Communities and Local Government, confirmed that 'The Government holds no statistics or estimates on the number or distribution of Slovak Roma, or Roma generally, in the UK' (Hansard Citation: HC Deb, 19 December 2012, c839W).

While the arrangements for data gathering could easily be resolved, a more challenging problem resides in the assumption that people will voluntarily identify their ethnicity. We know that Gypsy, Roma and Traveller individuals may often choose not to do so, against a background of historical oppression and hostility towards them and their identity (Cemlyn et al, 2009).

HISTORY OF OPPRESSION

There is a variety of work which examines the history of Gypsies, Roma and Travellers in great depth (Acton, 1974, 1994, 2000; Hawes and Perez, 1996; Acton and Mundy, 1997; Tong, 1998; Kenrick and Clark, 1999; and Hancock, 2002).

According to Kenrick and Clark's (1999) history, the Gypsies' presence in the UK in the early 16th century was initially welcomed. Seen as a useful mobile workforce, they became a valued source of labour who brought with them exotic traditions and exciting forms of entertainment. However, this initial acceptance was short-lived. Their nomadic tradition meant that Gypsies (and later other Traveller groups) quickly became targets of assimilatory practices in an effort to register them for the purposes of taxation. This attempt at state control was combined with religious leaders branding them as heretics (Kenrick and Clark, 1999). By 1530, growing public resentment towards Gypsies became manifest in the first statute of law expelling "Egyptians" from the UK. In 1562, the Act for the Punishment of Vagabonds Calling Themselves Egyptians made it a capital offence for anyone to be a Gypsy.

The 1572 Act for the Punishment of Vagabonds and for the Relief of the Poor and Impotent Poor meant that those who continued to travel were at risk of branding and slavery as the permitted forms of punishment for a nomadic lifestyle or culture. This Act also gave permission for Gypsy children to be "taken into service", thus witnessing one of the first legalised practices of removing Gypsy children from their families. As people attempted to survive this flood of anti-Gypsy legislation, they were forced to live in their small communities away from populated areas.

Although, by the 17th century, some anti-Gypsy laws were repealed – enabling Appleby Fair to be registered as a horse-trading fair in 1685 – the dominant trend was of the continued oppression of nomadic people. In 1822, the Turnpike Act was introduced and in 1908, the Children Act in England began to clamp down on travelling by making education for Gypsy children compulsory for half the year. Taking evidence from historical records, Liegeois (1986) shows how across Europe during this time, the forced sterilisation of women, torture, imprisonment and murder were all used in the process of achieving the same end – to eradicate the Gypsy culture, or cultural genocide.

Notwithstanding the unfavourable political context of the 19th century, various Gypsy and Traveller communities continued to play an important economic role in society. Engaging in seasonal agricultural work, such as pea or hop picking, working on the canals, or providing entertainment in various settings, families would travel the country, working and camping at the same places year after year, finding work and income for the community from scrap dealing, horse-trading, craftwork, etc.

Useful to the context being provided here, Richardson (2006) reminds us that during World War II, the Nazis drew up a list of Romani Gypsies for internment, and the holocaust of Gypsies in Europe is well documented (Kenrick and Clark, 1999). Whilst in the UK the Government did provide caravan sites for families of Gypsies fighting either overseas or working on the land, they closed these camps as soon as the war was over, forcing families once more to live in their small communities away from populated areas. In the period of mass industrialisation that followed the war, with the associated mechanisation and regulation of industry and agriculture, the opportunites for Gypsy, Roma and Traveller communities to find traditional work was reduced. For this reason, Gypsies and Travellers became an increasingly marginalised workforce.

In 1960, a key piece of legislation was introduced in the Caravan Sites and Control of Development Act. This Act is still significant as it effectively closed the commons and traditional stopping places of Gypsy and Traveller communities. However, rather than achieving the assimilation of these groups by forcing them to move them into bricks and mortar housing, the result was to create a shortage of sites, which once again caused community tensions as Gypsy and Traveller communities were forced to stay on pieces of land deemed by the majority community to be inappropriate, or private. In response to the crisis, Eric Lubbock's Private Member's Bill resulted in the 1968 Caravan Sites Act, which required local authorities to provide sites for Gypsies in England, but despite this statutory requirement, site development was slow.

Conflict between the state and the Gypsy, Roma and Traveller communities was highlighted again in the 1980s and 1990s in response to the growth of the New Traveller community, as evident in events like the "Battle of the Beanfield" or "Stonehenge Riots" (Worthington, 2005), which witnessed the forced removal of New Traveller children into care (Earle et al, 1994). In order to further restrict the travelling patterns of New Travellers and other Gypsy, Roma and Traveller groups, the 1994 Criminal Justice and Public Order Act criminalised unauthorised camping, and repealed many of the duties set out in the Caravan Sites Act.

Ryder and Greenfields (2010) explain that Gypsy, Roma and Traveller communities continue to face shortages of sustainable accommodation. Consistent with the history of Gypsy, Roma and Traveller communities in the UK, they also continue to face significant inequalities in access to education, health care, community support services, and social justice, and to experience a denial of their rights to family life.

Cemlyn et al (2009) highlight how these attacks have led to a considerable lack of contact and trust between Gypsy, Roma and Traveller families and formal agencies of state control. This suspicion, they report, is based on these material examples and a fear that their children will be taken into care. Evidence of the systematic removal of Gypsy, Roma and Traveller children as a strategy for "cultural genocide" in various countries in Europe is provided by Cemlyn and Briskman (2002) and others. There is evidence to show how the forceful removal of Gypsy, Roma and Traveller children has been common in Czechoslovakia (Guy, 1975), Italy (Mayall, 1995), Austria, France, Germany (Liegeois, 1994), Norway and Switzerland (Kenrick, 1994). Cemlyn and Briskman (2002) also explain that the threat of removal of children in the UK has been a routine strategy to control and harass Gypsies, Roma and Travellers. Okely (1983) also refers to the fear of child removal in England in the 1980s, and an Irish study showed the over-representation of Traveller children in care (O'Higgins, 1993).

On this basis, it is hardly surprising that some Gypsies, Roma or Travellers might conceal their ethnicity, as the fear of being identified by local authorities might result in the types of anti-Traveller treatment which Coxhead (2007) reports as being the "last bastion of racism". Although the "barbaric treatment" of Gypsies, Roma and Travellers has declined over time, Powell points out that the state continues 'to oppress the Gypsy, Roma and Traveller population through policies which have eroded cultural practices such as nomadism and the pursuit of traditional employment opportunities' (2007, p 121).

Fighting oppression

In recent times, the shared experiences of oppression and discrimination have led some Gypsy, Roma and Traveller communities to unite in their struggle for equality. Some communities have also come together in campaigns and organisations, such as the Gypsy Council, the Traveller Law Reform Coalition and the Irish Traveller Movement in Britain, which have managed to create a momentum for a degree of cultural and political recognition.

3

Social policy context

The history of oppression experienced by Gypsy, Roma and Traveller people has been underpinned by an ideology of assimilation driven by the dominant community over a number of generations. For many Gypsy, Roma and Traveller families, the experience of disadvantage, oppression and marginalisation have often been as the result of enforced settlement (Fraser, 1995; Cemlyn and Briskman, 2002; Vanderbeck, 2005) with nomadism arguably being perceived as a threat to dominant economic and political interests (McVeigh, 1997). In a capitalist society, the presence of a nomadic people has been seen as problematic, primarily because their economic activity could not be easily taxed, and other aspects of their lives could not be easily monitored and controlled.

The historical context in Europe includes episodes of systematic removal of Gypsy, Roma and Traveller children from their families in order to "eradicate Gypsy existence and culture" (Cemlyn and Briskman, 2002; Liegeois, 1986) and in the UK less systematic but nevertheless harmful approaches have been commonplace (Cemlyn *et al*, 2009). Such practices have not only been deeply damaging for individuals and families but have threatened the cultural survival of the group. In looking at all aspects of social policy, it is important to understand the political ideology that underpins this – an ideology that has excluded or ignored Gypsy, Roma and Traveller people, or active state discrimination and racism which, for the most part, has gone unchallenged.

ACCOMMODATION

As a result of ongoing prejudice and political hostility, many Gypsy, Roma and Traveller communities face significant challenges in practising the nomadic traditions which were fundamental in their recognition, and subsequent protection, as ethnic minorities. Despite the legal requirement and duty to protect their cultural heritage, local authorities that might continue to build or procure social housing are less likely to build or procure social campsites. As a result of this discrimination and the associated significant shortages in social accommodation, one-half to two-thirds of the Gypsy and Traveller population are currently in bricks-and-mortar housing (Shelter, 2008). While the majority of those living in caravans are on authorised public or private sites (Brown and Niner, 2009), up to a fifth of caravan-dwelling families who are unable to access authorised sites live on unauthorised encampments or by the roadside (Greenfields and Smith, 2010).

Authorised camps

Authorised camps are generally seen as either those sites owned and operated by local authorities, or those owned by families and communities and which have planning permission for the buildings, hard standing, stables, outhouses and so on which may have been built there.

Although the Government has allocated substantial sums to local housing authorities to develop new sites or refurbish old ones, the extent to which local authorities and registered social landlords access such grants varies considerably across areas and is often dependent upon political will and changing local circumstances (Richardson *et al*, 2010). Furthermore, many of the sites that are owned and operated by local authorities are of poor quality, and compound health risks through inadequate sewage and water fittings, poor-quality utility rooms, and failings in fire safety.

For these reasons, private site development is still preferred by many (Richardson *et al*, 2010), but securing planning permission for a Gypsy, Roma and Traveller-owned site can be extremely difficult. Already strict planning legislation can be compounded by anti-Traveller racism and active opposition from local residents resulting in applications being turned down, especially when opposition is accompanied by public protests. This means that although the majority of those living in caravans are on authorised public or private sites, there is not enough authorised accommodation to meet the demand (Brown and Niner, 2009).

Unauthorised camps

As a direct result of the shortages in authorised accommodation, many Gypsy, Roma and Traveller families have no choice but to stop in places that are far from ideal, and where they have no permission, such as highway verges, derelict land, open spaces, recreation grounds, forestland, lay-bys, and car parks (Greenfields and Smith, 2010). Tighter and more strictly enforced planning and trespass laws, combined with the enclosure and utilisation of a great deal of wasteland, has much diminished the opportunities for short stops. If Gypsy, Roma and Travellers camp on any ground without a relevant planning certificate or the landowner's permission, they are, by definition, breaking the law.

Furthermore, using such places often means restricted access to running water, sanitation and refuse collection. Also, by the nature of the fact that they are considered homeless, this brings difficulties in accessing public services like education, health and social care. Those living on unauthorised sites will usually also find no safe play space for children, no sense of security, and will live with the constant fear of harassment and vigilante attacks.

There is also the risk of eviction. There are various ways in which landowners can evict Gypsy, Roma and Travellers families, and most commonly private bailiffs are employed to move people on. In some cases, the landowner petitions the court and receives a notice of eviction, but if a criminal offence has taken place, the police can take eviction action. Resulting from this lack of provision, as many as one-fifth of the caravan-dwelling population is homeless as they have nowhere legal to park a caravan (Cemlyn *et al*, 2009). This also extends to those people living on canals and rivers specifically linked to policy changes in relation to home moorings (see Environment, Food and Rural Affairs Committee, 2012).

Living in a house

In the absence of adequate authorised provision, and in order to avoid the stresses and anxieties that come with living on unauthorised sites or moorings, many families avoid what Cemlyn *et al* (2009, p v) describe as the "eviction cycle" by reluctantly moving into bricks-and-mortar housing. However, when this decision is made, families can be exposed to more direct and immediate forms of public hostility focused on their ethnicity or lifestyle. As this decision often involves dislocation from their wider communities, culture, and support systems, families are reported to encounter further cycles of disadvantage, oppression and marginalisation (Lau and Ridge, 2011). It is important to be clear that just because someone from a Gypsy, Roma and Traveller background has moved into bricks-and-mortar housing, this does not mean that they have ceased to be members of the Gypsy, Roma and Traveller community.

Symbolism of the house

Allen (2013) has shown that for some Gypsies and Travellers the experience of moving into bricks-and-mortar accommodation can result in a sense of culture shock. For some, the "house" can come to represent a form of control, a symbol of forced assimilation, which reflects those structural inequalities that have threatened Gypsy and Traveller freedoms throughout the centuries. The significance of this for children being taken into care should not be underestimated because the symbolism of a "house" can sometimes be overlooked. In addition to the experiences of separation and loss, the building itself can become a powerful representation of a loss of culture, heritage and tradition. Where this is the case, some Gypsy and Traveller children might find it difficult to come to terms with their new situation.

EDUCATION

In addition to the challenges faced by Gypsy, Roma and Traveller families in accommodation, there is also much evidence of severe and continuing discrimination in relation to education and, according to Ofsted (1999), Gypsy, Roma and Traveller children are 'the groups most at risk in the education system'. In large part, this is the result of services being designed for the majority population, and therefore not meeting the needs of a nomadic lifestyle or recognising other cultural values. This is compounded by the unavailability of adequate accommodation that means education is disrupted when children move on, or are moved on.

Historically, it has often not been possible for Gypsy, Roma and Traveller children to attend school as this has been incompatible with a nomadic lifestyle, or because of discrimination by the education authorities. Kiddle (2000) reports the experience of Mary Delaney, who came to national attention in 1977 when she was refused a school place because she came from an unauthorised site.

Today, the majority of Gypsy, Roma and Traveller parents want their children to go to primary school to learn to read and write, but for some parents education at secondary school level can be seen as a threat to Gypsy, Roma and Traveller culture, especially when topics such as sex education are being discussed (Bhopal, 2011). In light of strict mores in relation to the separate socialisation of girls and boys (see Chapter 4), Bhopal suggests that some parents and communities believe that mixing too much with the majority society would mean that their child could "lose their sense of identity", and for this reason can see secondary schooling as undesirable.

Although good work has been done by some schools, the Traveller Education Support Services, and other specific projects to provide an equal and inclusive education, some children can still find that their culture is ignored within the education system. For those Gypsy, Roma and Traveller children who attend school, it is widely reported that they encounter bullying from other children and that their school may also be located in a hostile neighbourhood. Whilst the experience of Mary Delaney occurred in the 1970s, there are more recent reported cases where schools have been closed or threatened with closure when Gypsy, Roma and Traveller children were enrolled because other parents mounted a campaign against them and withdrew their children (Bhopal, 2011).

Travellers Education Support Service

The Travellers Education Support Service works with Gypsy, Roma and Traveller families to:

- provide advice and support to schools regarding the inclusion of pupils from Traveller families;

- provide advice and support to Traveller families regarding admission to school and attendance.

The Travellers Education Support Service aims to help local education authorities fulfil their statutory duty in relation to Gypsy, Roma and Traveller children and their families in a variety of educational settings. However, funding for the future of this specialist education resource is currently under review. Whilst some Traveller Education Support Services remain, this once vibrant national support service is now very much diminished.

HEALTH

A major study for the Department of Health found that Gypsy, Roma and Traveller communities had significantly poorer physical health, and significantly more self-reported symptoms of ill-health, than the population at large. According to the British Medical Association, Gypsy and Traveller communities have the lowest life expectancy and highest rate of child mortality in Britain (Parry *et al*, 2004). These concerns are often directly correlated to poverty and the poor living conditions that this group experience, compounded by unequal access to health services. Prejudice, communication difficulties with health staff, and the frequent experience of eviction, even when family members are receiving medical treatment, all serve to exacerbate the problem.

Lau and Ridge (2011) have noted that because Gypsy, Roma and Traveller culture and identity often receive inadequate recognition within education, health, or social services, many Gypsy, Roma and Traveller people experience consequent and considerable oppression which can significantly damage their self-esteem. Shelter (2008) also reports that there is a substantial negative psychological impact on Gypsy, Roma and Traveller children who experience repeated brutal evictions. This extends to family tensions associated with insecure lifestyles, and an unending stream of overt and extreme hostility from the wider population (Warrington, 2006).

In addition to the experience of insecurity and hostility, there is an increasing problem of substance abuse among unemployed and disaffected young Gypsy, Roma and Traveller people (Joseph Rowntree Foundation, 2007). It is widely held that people who are socially excluded in employment terms are also disproportionately likely to experience poor physical and mental health (Cummins *et al*, 2005) and consistent with this concern there are high suicide rates in Gypsy, Roma and Traveller communities (van Cleemput, 2004).

SOCIAL WORK

Social work values promote anti-discriminatory practice, while the development of equality legislation has meant there is a legal obligation to provide culturally appropriate services for a diverse service user group (see Chapter 5). However, findings from the available research into the experiences of Gypsies and Travellers with social work services demonstrate that these commitments and duties remain significantly unfulfilled, with little proactive policy at governmental or local authority level, and fragmented attempts by individual social workers (Cemlyn, 1998). As with other minority groups (Penketh, 2000), but sometimes with more severe manifestations, Gypsies, Roma and Travellers may experience an excess of controlling intervention and a lack of supportive services. An early monograph discussed low levels of engagement between Gypsies and social services, including a 'de facto conspiracy to ignore Gypsies' (Butler, 1983, p 26), while in contrast other studies have highlighted over-intervention and the trauma of children being systematically removed from their families, thereby threatening their cultural identity (Okely, 1983).

Subsequent studies have found that the fear associated with this historical community experience, together with the hostile context for Gypsy, Roma and Traveller communities, and uncertainty, fear and hesitation on the part of social workers, perpetuate problematic relationships (Cemlyn, 2000a; Garrett, 2004a; Power, 2004). Cemlyn (2000b) found that intervention mainly took the form of crisis response in child protection and youth justice, with a lack of community engagement or preventive work, leading to further alienation, mistrust and damage. The lack of awareness and understanding of the communities could lead to a failure even of a crisis response to meet urgent needs, with Power (2004) referring to 'institutional blindness'. Further barriers to access to supportive services include:

- organisational failure to respond to frequent movement of families, with services geared to the majority population;

- an absence of accessible, realistic information about services;

- ignorance of or prejudice about Gypsy and Traveller culture, including a lack of awareness of minority ethnic status, and lack of attention to wider issues facing Gypsies and Travellers (Cemlyn, 2000b; Greenfields, 2002; 2006; Power, 2004); and

- involvement in surveillance and control of Gypsy and Traveller lifestyles through assessments in relation to eviction (Cemlyn, 2000a; 2008; Cowan and Lomax, 2003; Garrett, 2004).

Studies have also identified some positive developments in the form of occasional specialist teams or projects, and individual social work initiatives (Cemlyn, 2000b; Power, 2004; Garrett, 2005); a few local authorities taking proactive children's rights stances in relation to responses to unauthorised camping (Cemlyn, 2000a); sensitive attempts by Scottish social workers to engage appropriately with the 'shifting marginalised identities' of housed Travellers (Morran, 2002); and other more anecdotal evidence of efforts to work positively with Gypsy and Traveller families and communities.

CRIMINAL JUSTICE

There is widespread stereotyping of the Gypsy, Roma and Traveller communities as being engaged in criminal activity (Power, 2004; James, 2005; Greenfields, 2006); one study (Dawson, 2000) describes how this is expressed through public and media allegations of rises in crime when Travellers enter a neighbourhood, despite evidence to the contrary.

The suspicion with which Gypsy, Roma and Traveller communities can be regarded means that they are likely to experience unequal treatment from the police and cite stories of being arrested without due cause, being unfairly barred from public venues, or being repeatedly stopped and questioned (Pizani Williams, 1996). The unequal treatment and attention from police has resulted in disproportionate levels of Anti-Social Behaviour Orders (ASBOs), high use of remand in custody, and prejudice within pre-sentence reports (Power, 2004). As noted in relation to housing, cultural dislocation within the prison system can also lead to acute distress and frequently suicide (Wired, 2005; MacGabhann, 2011).

INVISIBILITY

A discussion of these issues is incomplete without acknowledging the invisibility of Gypsy, Roma and Traveller communities in the social policy discourse, and recognising that the disregard of their perspectives within social care literature has been a factor in the way social policy has developed (Allen, 2012).

In the absence of a Gypsy, Roma and Traveller voice, Allen (2012) argues that social policies are embedded within the values and expectations of the dominant culture, and serve to exclude Gypsy, Roma and Traveller communities. Policy initiatives designed to promote inclusion, such as community development and community cohesion programmes, frequently exclude Gypsy, Roma and Traveller communities, resulting in a dearth of culturally appropriate support services for people in the most vulnerable situations.

Where efforts have been made to recognise minority ethnic groups in policy, this has tended to emphasise a common experience of oppression, favouring the term "Black and Minority Ethnic" as a "catch-all" label. This serves to mask the specific, and has arguably made the experiences of Gypsy, Roma and Traveller communities invisible, giving the impression that their specific needs are being considered, when in fact very often they are not.

Ethnicity, cultures, traditions and beliefs

In reading this chapter, it is essential to understand that it aims to offer broad generalisations about some Gypsy, Roma and Traveller groups. It does not apply equally to all members of any Gypsy, Roma and Traveller community, and is in no way meant to be a substitute for finding more information about specific family culture and mores when working with Gypsy, Roma and Traveller families. This cannot be emphasised strongly enough. There are nevertheless some advantages to this discussion of traditions and beliefs; if for no other reason than to dispel some of the myths and misunderstandings that undoubtedly exist.

A number of important texts have been written by Gypsy, Roma and Traveller people specifically for this purpose. Jake Bowers, one of Britain's very few Romani journalists, has written a number of information packs for readers who are not part of these communities. His publication *Guide to Working with Gypsies and Travellers* (2009), written specifically for social workers, is an important publication for anyone wishing to develop their understanding of the challenges that exist. The works of Ceija Stojka, a Roma writer and artist; Jess Smith, a Scottish Traveller; Maggie Bendell Smith, a Romani Gypsy; Michael McDonagh, an Irish Traveller; and Nan Joyce, an Irish Traveller, are also essential for those wishing to develop a deeper understanding of some of the topics that this practice guide presents. Another resource is the Leeds GATE (Gypsy and Traveller Exchange) publication entitled *How to Engage with Gypsies and Travellers as Part of your Work*, which is also available as a CD-ROM (see Useful organisations for contact details of Leeds GATE). It is important to point out that the majority of the summaries presented below have been taken from these sources.

NOMADISM

The tradition of nomadism or "travelling" is a central tenet of Gypsy and Traveller cultures, serving economic and social purposes throughout history, and being a common denominator in their experience. Within this tradition, some communities will regularly meet up for weddings, christenings and funerals, and maintain their traditions through seasonal travelling. For some, travelling is simply the norm, and to do anything else feels unnatural and restrictive. Some families who live in houses may hold a desire to travel again (see Parry *et al*, 2004), whilst for others living in a house is perfectly acceptable.

It is important to be clear that even if people are unable to travel because of illness or social circumstances, or because they have chosen to settle in a house or permanent campsite, they still retain their ethnicity and position in their communities. Being nomadic is *not* the defining characteristic of what it means to be a Gypsy, Roma or Traveller. For Liegeois (1986, p 53), travelling is 'more a state of mind than an actual situation' and in the modern world, it is more difficult than ever to adhere to traditional ways.

ETHNICITY

In cases since 1989, it has been established through the courts that the customs and traditions of Romani Gypsies (*Commission for Racial Equality v Dutton*, 1989), Irish Travellers (*O'Leary and others v Punch Retail and others*, 2000), and Scottish Gypsy/Travellers (*MacLennan v Gypsy Traveller Education and Information Project*, 2008) should be protected under equality legislation. In order to secure this political and legal recognition, it was necessary for each of these groups to demonstrate that they experience discrimination on the grounds of "race" and ethnicity, and to demonstrate against the "Mandla Criteria" that being Romani Gypsies, Irish Travellers, and Scottish Gypsy/Traveller is a matter of cultural heritage, rather than a lifestyle choice (see Chapter 5 for more detail on the legal context). For this reason, the words Gypsy, Roma and Traveller should be spelt with upper-case letters to signify their status as distinct ethnic groups, and good practice demands the same approach for other specific travelling communities.

The "Mandla Criteria"

Mandla and another v Dowell Lee and another, 1983, concerned a Sikh boy who was refused entry to a school because he refused to stop wearing a turban or cut his hair. After a complaint to the Commission for Racial Equality, the case was taken to court, and under the resultant "Mandla Criteria" the court established the issues that were relevant in considering the existence of an ethnic group, such as:

- a long shared history;

- a cultural tradition of their own;

- a common geographical origin;

- a common language;

- a common religion.

PRIDE IN FAMILY AND COMMUNITY

Gypsy and Traveller communities tend to share a belief in the importance of family and community. For many travelling people there is a mutual reliance on extended family, for both practical and emotional support. There is also a commitment to family across the generations, with Gypsy, Roma and Traveller communities expecting to care for their elders. Rites of passage such as christenings, weddings, illness and funerals are very important events that allow for large gatherings of extended families and communities, and serve to maintain membership of distinct ethnic or cultural groups.

Gypsy, Roma and Traveller groups would not have survived centuries of oppression without a pride in being Gypsy, Roma or Traveller, and without fighting against assimilation attempts in many guises. However, the importance of the survival of relatively small ethnic or cultural populations usually requires an ideology that excludes some aspects of the majority society which can be perceived as a threat to traditional mores (Okley, 1983; Allen, 2013). What this means in a Gypsy, Roma and Traveller context is that it might be difficult for those individuals who are not perceived to be culturally "pure" to be seen as fully integrated members of the Gypsy, Roma and Traveller community.

For some Gypsy, Roma or Traveller parents, this is very much reflected in their thinking about secondary education, where risks of socialisation with the "contaminating" dominant group are seen to be a justifiable reason for not promoting education for older children. Such attitudes will also impact on those individuals from the community who either inter-marry with people from the majority community, or who are brought up in care outside of the Gypsy, Roma and Traveller communities. For others in these communities, such attitudes may be seen as old-fashioned, or as changing in the context of an economic climate where self-employment in traditional manual work becomes less achievable.

Being "half radge"

"Half radge" is a derogatory term that is used by some in the Romani community to describe other Romani people who are considered to be settled. Use of this label suggests a discriminatory hierarchy within some Romani communities that values the "purity" of ancestry and the continued survival of certain "in-group" mores through strictly governed socialisations. It also reflects a number of value judgements about settled people and their cultures.

Being labelled "half radge" can present many barriers in terms of social inclusion and social equality, and clearly has implications for children who are brought up in the care system by carers from the majority community. For women in particular, being labelled "half radge" has implications in terms of reputation around sexual innocence, and risks them being discriminated against as "dirty" and unsuitable for marriage in the Romani community.

For Irish Travellers, the term "gorgio" (other spellings exist) carries the same meaning and will have similar implications.

RELIGION

Cemlyn *et al* (2009) explain that religion can be of great importance to many Gypsy, Roma and Traveller individuals, and this is evident in ritual gatherings as well as day-to-day life. They explain that Irish Travellers are often devout Roman Catholics and many will go on pilgrimages to Lourdes or holy places in Ireland. Romani Gypsies are more likely to be born-again Christians who will meet with others at Christian conventions across Europe.

CLEANLINESS AND HYGIENE

Contrary to some widely held stereotypical views, Gypsy, Roma and Traveller individuals and families have strict cultural norms in relation to cleanliness and hygiene, but these are based on different ideas to those of the majority community.

> We never wash in a sink. If we have a sink in the trailer it's always got a dish inside, 'cos we have separate bowls for everything...for washing up...for washing our hands and face...and for wiping around. We never get 'em mixed up. When we are doing our laundry we won't wash our tea towels in with all the rest of our clothes, 'cos we think that's very unclean.
>
> (Gypsy Anna Lee quoted in Saunders *et al*, 2000)

Some Gypsies, Roma and Travellers may also never put anything that has been on the floor (such as a bag) on the table, and will take great pride in cleaning their trailers, even in the challenging context of having limited water, or being routinely evicted and moved on.

ANIMALS AND LIVESTOCK

Animals and livestock are an important part of Gypsy, Roma and Traveller life, as reflected in the important role of horse-trading and horse fairs today. Research by Exchange House Travellers Service (2004) has shown that because horses are such a large part of some Gypsy, Roma and Traveller cultures, young people in families with a horse can routinely spend 18 hours per week with their horse or riding their sulky (a lightweight cart with two wheels and a seat for the driver). Such is the importance of this cultural practice that the Exchange House Travellers Service in Ireland (2004) indicates that a young person growing up in a horse-owning family is less at risk of becoming involved in substance misuse and crime.

GENDER ROLES AND SEXUALITY

Ryder and Greenfields (2010) explain that the nature of some Gypsy, Roma and Traveller cultures means that access to work usually occurs informally from within the family unit. Amongst many families, the traditional employment of young people within a family-run business has long been the ideal form of economic activity. Thus, Derrington and Kendal (2004) suggest that individuals (particularly men) who are able to make a living and support their family using traditional skills are often seen within the community as being successful. Whilst this may be positive for the development of a male identity, this can potentially lead to heavily gendered roles and expectations of families. Thus, women are largely expected to focus on domestic or "home-based" roles or supporting activities which enable men to work outside the home (Levinson and Sparkes, 2003).

Whilst Gypsy, Roma and Traveller women have suffered because of high levels of social exclusion (Cemlyn *et al*, 2009), they have been more adept than males at coping with social change. So successful have many women been at making a transition to new economic activities that Levinson and Sparkes (2003) report a growing defensiveness around Gypsy, Roma and Traveller gender roles. Indeed, there have been reports of growing tensions within families where changes have occurred to traditional Gypsy and Traveller gendered roles and women have become more involved in external employment activities (Richardson *et al*, 2007).

Whilst these tensions may become manifest in many ways, the most significant concern relates to high instances of domestic abuse within some families. A presentation by Roberts and colleagues (2007) on the health of Gypsies and Travellers in Wrexham, for instance, reported that 61 per cent of married English Gypsy women and 81 per cent of married Irish Traveller women interviewed for the study had experienced domestic abuse.

Domestic abuse is also a concern where young Traveller and Gypsy women stand accused of sexual promiscuity. Where reported, promiscuity can provide a cultural justification to alienate women under charges that they have been "contaminated" by majority society cultural pressures. As sexual liberality on the part of women is judged to conflict with Gypsy, Roma and Traveller norms, including a notion of sexual purity, any such behaviour by young women is seen to bring shame onto a family, and jeopardise the cultural survival of the group (Parker-Jenkins and Hartas, 2002; Derrington and Kendall, 2004; O'Hanlon and Holmes, 2004; Power, 2004; Bhopal, 2011). The punishments for subverting cultural ideology, reported by Pavee Point (2005) and Nexus (2006), often take the form of "in-group" violence, abuse, social castigation and exile.

The concept of gender equality also extends to sexual equality. The limited references which do exist in regard to this generally relate to homophobic responses to Traveller and Gypsy young people who do not wish to marry, or who explain to family and community members that they might be lesbian, gay, bisexual, or transgender (see, for example, Cemlyn *et al*, 2009). Gypsy and Traveller people who disclose minority sexuality are seen to be influenced by the views of the majority population, which are believed to promote unacceptable sexual liberality (Okely, 1983).

Attitudes to gender

Reflecting on their experiences of living in care as children, Irish Travellers Lisa, Emma and Sarah describe gender differences in Traveller and non-Traveller families:

Emma: *Yeah, like you're not allowed to go over and speak to a group of boys even if they are your cousins because you're not allowed. If you're brought up within a settled family, you're going to act a lot and get a lot of Travellers going, like, 'They have too much freedom,' whereas here you're kind of brought up better and you kind of...*

Sarah: *I think that if a Traveller child was put with a settled family, their rearing is going to be completely different. Even if they are there for a couple of years, they are going to be used to a lot more freedom whereas children with Travelling families are going to learn a lot of the Traveller values, and that helps Travellers marry other Travellers so that it keeps the culture going so...*

Lisa: *Yeah, boys have more freedom. We have lived with two other Traveller foster brothers and they are treated a lot different. That's just the way it is. Girls are meant to be seen and not heard. Do you ever watch* Pride and Prejudice? *(Laughing) It's just like that. Men are, like, not superior but they are allowed to speak up but we are not. We are very guarded...*

(Allen, 2013)

PRIVACY AND ATTITUDES TO AUTHORITY

There is an expectation in some communities that inter-familial difficulties are private matters within the family, and should be dealt with accordingly. This can lead to communities being reluctant to involve outside agencies in issues such as domestic violence, substance misuse and ill health.

The need for community privacy is important because the involvement of social workers and police can be seen to bring unwanted attention. This means that some individuals and groups within the wider Gypsy, Roma and Traveller community can struggle to seek help from people or organisations perceived to be outside of the group's internal social network. In light of the generations of persecution and marginalisation that Gypsy, Roma and Traveller communities have experienced from the majority community, some still view police, social workers and other agents of the state with a deep sense of mistrust. Given the historical context and current socio-economic relationships, this attitude is entirely understandable, but at times this reluctance to engage with authority can result in unhelpful denial and secrecy. Understanding the relationship between the state and the Gypsy, Roma and Traveller communities is central to working with this group in relation to children, and this theme runs throughout this good practice guide.

Denial and secrecy: children being taken into care

Irish Traveller and human rights activist Ruth talks about the apparent denial that any Traveller or Gypsy child would ever have to go into care, the denial and secrecy that comes with this, and the impact on those who have lived in care.

Ruth: *I try and talk to families about the Traveller and Gypsy children who are in care, and people look at me sideways and say that a Traveller child would never go into care because the family would always step in to take care of them. For them, the idea that a Traveller child could go into care is absurd. But it's true, Traveller children do go into care because the problems that you have are the same problems that we have. In fact, our problems are worse because everything is hush-hush. Going into care is seen as a terrible thing. Every woman you speak to would say that they would never let their own child into care. But it happens. I get angry when people say, oh, Traveller children never go into care. I did. If the community were that concerned about children they would have never let me go into care, but they did and I think, well, what was different about me? If you are that protective, why didn't you protect me?*

(Allen, 2013)

The law and social work with children

There are three sets of provisions which affect and should support all children across the UK, including children in Gypsy, Roma and Traveller communities:

- European Convention on Human Rights (ECHR), incorporated into UK law by the Human Rights Act 1998;

- equalities/anti-discrimination legislation; and

- United Nations Convention on the Rights of the Child (UNCRC).

European Convention on Human Rights (ECHR)

All children and all communities in the UK are covered by the ECHR which applies equally to children and adults. Gypsy, Roma and Traveller children, families and communities are as entitled to the same protection under these provisions as everyone else. All public authorities are bound by the ECHR, including courts, local authorities and Health Boards in Northern Ireland. The main relevant articles for looked after children and other children and families are article 8 (a right to respect for private and family life); and article 6 (a right to a fair hearing when decisions are made about civil or criminal rights).

Articles 3 and 5 may also be relevant. Article 3 is the right not to be subjected to torture or degrading treatment; this will be relevant if the care conditions for children and young people are poor and inadequate. Article 5 is the right to liberty and security and will be relevant if children and young people are detained or secured wrongly.

Equalities/anti-discrimination legislation

The equality legislation for England, Wales and Scotland is now in the Equality Act 2010, which requires that all children who are looked after should be cared for in a way that respects, recognises, supports and celebrates their identity and provides them with care, support and opportunities to maximise their individual potential.

In Northern Ireland, the relevant equalities legislation is the Race Relations (Northern Ireland) Order 1997, as amended, and this specifically recognises the "Irish Traveller community".

In cases since 1989 (see box on following page), it has been established that the customs and traditions of Romany Gypsies, Irish Travellers and Scottish Gypsy/Travellers should be protected. To secure this political and legal recognition, it was necessary for each of these groups to demonstrate that they had experienced discrimination on the grounds of "race" and ethnicity, and to demonstrate with reference to the "Mandla Criteria" (see Chapter 4) that being Romany Gypsies, Irish Travellers and Scottish Gypsy/Travellers is a matter of cultural heritage, rather than a lifestyle choice.

The relevance of this for local authorities and others is that since Romany Gypsies, Irish Travellers and Scottish Gypsy/Travellers are now recognised as specific minority ethnic groups, they should receive the full protection of the law in terms of equality and inclusion. And although some Gypsy, Roma and Traveller communities are not yet formally recognised in law as being ethnic groups, many of the same arguments apply to their situations. It is therefore appropriate to treat all Gypsy, Roma and Traveller groups as minority ethnic groups, with all that implies in terms of the principles laid down in equality legislation and duty.

Case law

Commission for Racial Equality v Dutton (1989)

In this case, pub landlord Mr Dutton displayed signs stating "No Travellers", after claiming that Travellers from a local illegal site were causing trouble for him and his regular customers. The Commission for Racial Equality was alerted to this matter and brought the case against Mr Dutton. The court found that the term Travellers included Romani Gypsies, and that Romani Gypsies were a minority group with a shared history and geographical origin with certain customs, languages, folktales and music of their own. As such, it was concluded that they should be deemed a minority racial group under the Race Relations Act 1976 (as amended in 2000), and not be discriminated against.

O'Leary and Others v Punch Retail and others (2000)

In this case, Irish Travellers had been refused service in a number of pubs in London, and the preliminary issue to be determined was whether they constituted a distinct racial group for the purposes of the Race Relations Act 1976. After a six-day hearing, it was concluded that they were.

MacLennan v Gypsy Traveller Education and Information Project (2008)

Mr MacLennan, who had been employed and then dismissed as strategic co-ordinator with the Gypsy Traveller Education and Information Project in Aberdeen, claimed that he had been victimised in relation to the stance he took over the closure of a lay-by to Scottish Gypsy/Travellers and a child protection case involving a Scottish Gypsy/Traveller. He complained of unfair dismissal and victimisation under the Race Relations Act 1976 (as amended in 2000). In October 2008, an employment appeal tribunal overturned the finding of an earlier tribunal and ruled that Scottish Gypsy/Travellers were a separate ethnic group under the Race Relations Act.

United Nations Convention on the Rights of the Child (UNCRC)

In addition to the ECHR and equalities legislation, the four UK countries are committed to the principles set out in the United Nations Convention on the Rights of the Child 1989 (see box overleaf). These are relevant to children from Gypsy, Roma and Traveller communities, as they are for all children. The UNCRC principles have been increasingly reflected in legislation for children across the UK, although the Convention itself is not fully incorporated into law in the same way as the ECHR. However, the principles are very important and relevant to decisions by public authorities and courts. They are persuasive in court cases and often referred to in judgements relating to children.

United Nations Convention on the Rights of the Child (UNCRC) (1989)

All legislation across the UK should seek to be compliant with the UNCRC, and a number of articles are particularly relevant to work with Gypsy, Roma and Traveller children, including those quoted below:

- Article 3 – All organisations concerned with children should work towards what is best for each child.

- Article 12 – Children have the right to say what they think should happen when adults are making decisions that affect them, and to have their opinions taken into account.

- Article 16 – Children have a right to privacy. The law should protect them from attacks against their way of life, their good name, their families and their homes.

- Article 20 – Children who cannot be looked after by their own family must be looked after properly, by people who respect their religion, culture and language.

- Article 29 – Education...should encourage children to respect their parents, and their own and other cultures.

- Article 30 – Children have a right to learn and use the language and customs of their families, whether these are shared by the majority of people in the country or not.

IMPLICATIONS FOR CHILDREN IN CARE

The equality requirements set out above mean that every individual child who is looked after should be cared for in a way that respects, recognises, supports and celebrates their identity. However, despite this statutory requirement, growing evidence suggests that Gypsies, Roma and Traveller children in public care experience wide-ranging inequalities (O'Higgins, 1993; Pemberton, 1999; Scottish Parliament, 2012; Allen, 2013).

In terms of foster care provision, Cemlyn (2000b) explains that there is almost no evidence of any proactive work to recruit Gypsy, Roma and Traveller foster carers, or to train other foster carers and adopters in this specific area of need. What this means is that when these children enter into care, they are likely to be placed in foster placements or residential homes away from their own culture, and alienated from their community networks. Supporting this claim, Father Gerard Barry, a chaplain at HM Prison, Full Sutton, summarised in Cemlyn et al (2009), reported that:

There is evidence that if a decision is made to have a Traveller child taken into care, then no effort is made to find a Traveller family to care for them – quite contrary to the normal practice of trying to find a family best suited to a child's cultural background.

(p 128)

The following sections set out the specific legal requirements for practice around ethnicity and culture with children in care in the four UK countries.

England

Where a child cannot live with a birth parent, the Children Act 1989 (as amended by the Children and Young Persons Act 2008) requires local authorities to 'give preference to' a placement with a person who is a relative, friend or other connected person, and the Public Law Outline requires authorities to consider family members and friends as potential carers at each stage of the decision-making process. For Gypsy, Roma and Traveller children, this inevitably means considering as carers members of the Gypsy, Roma and Traveller community of which they are a part.

For children who are looked after by a local authority, there are specific provisions within the child care legislation and guidance in relation to promoting racial, religious and cultural equality. Section 22(5) of the Children Act 1989 provides that decisions concerning children being looked after shall 'take into account the child's religious persuasion, racial origin and cultural and linguistic background'. This provision is supported by the Care Planning, Placement and Case Review Regulations (2010) which require these same matters to be considered at each review meeting.

The Fostering Services Statutory Guidance in England (2011) provides the following more detailed requirements in relation to meeting the identity needs of children in foster care, all of which have relevance in working with children from Gypsy, Roma and Traveller communities:

3.44. *Foster carers and fostering services should ensure that full attention is paid to the individual child's gender, faith, ethnic origin, cultural and linguistic background, sexual orientation and any disability they might have. Children should be encouraged and supported to have positive views of themselves and to be proud of their identity and heritage (standard 2).*

3.46. *Foster carers should be informed, trained and confident about dealing with issues relating to gender, religion, ethnic origin, cultural background, linguistic background, nationality, disability or sexual orientation, and be able to involve external professional advice and support as necessary.*

3.47. Foster carers should be supported to help individual children and young people cope if they are subject to discrimination, marginalisation or ridicule from their peers by virtue of their gender, religion, ethnic origin, cultural background, linguistic background, nationality, disability, sexual orientation or looked after status.

3.48. Cultural, racial, faith based or ethnic expectations about [children's] clothing or diet should be met and supported.

In terms of education, the 1996 Education Act requires parents to provide education for their children 'either by regular attendance at school or otherwise', and for those families who travel, dual registration enables children to be registered at more than one school. This protects Gypsy, Roma or Traveller children from being deleted from the register of their "base" school while they are attending elsewhere (Department for Education, 2012).

The rights of Gypsy, Roma and Traveller children are also addressed in the European Framework Convention for the Protection of Minorities 1995, which is binding on members of the Council of Europe. Article 12 refers to state parties taking 'measures in the fields of education and research to foster knowledge of the culture, history, language and religion of their national minorities and of the majority', to providing adequate opportunities for teacher training, and 'equal opportunities for access to education at all levels for persons belonging to national minorities'.

Wales

The Children Act 1989 also applies in Wales, bringing the same requirement to both identify suitable family or friends carers for children unable to live with birth parents, and to take into account the looked after child's 'religious persuasion, racial origin and cultural and linguistic background'. The Act is supplemented by the following regulations:

- Fostering Services (Wales) Regulations 2003

- Placement of Children (Wales) Regulations 2007

- Review of Children's Cases (Wales) Regulations 2007

These provisions give some guidance on the types of services which should be provided to meet the diversity of children's needs arising from culture, language and religion, and provide a series of instructions on how to deal robustly and sensitively with issues of prejudice, inequality, discrimination and oppression. The Education Act 1996 applies to both England and Wales, and further guidance around educational matters is provided in *Moving Forward: Gypsy and Traveller education* (Welsh Assembly Government Circular no: 003/2008).

Scotland

The Children (Scotland) Act 1995 requires that local authorities, courts and others must take account of children's 'religious persuasion, racial origin and cultural and linguistic background' when working with, planning for and making decisions about the children. This applies whether children are living in their communities or are away from home, temporarily or permanently. When children cannot remain at home, it is good legal and welfare practice for local authorities to try to work with and consider arrangements with their extended families or communities, where that is compatible with the children's welfare.

These are general duties under the child care legislation which apply to work with Gypsy, Roma and Traveller children and families as to all others. The main relevant provisions are the Children (Scotland) Act 1995, the Adoption and Children (Scotland) Act 2007 and the Children's Hearings (Scotland) Act 2011. For looked after children and those for whom local authorities are considering adoption, there are also the Looked after Children (Scotland) Regulations 2009 and the Adoption Agencies (Scotland) Regulations 2009.

All these provisions set out the framework for local authority and adoption agency duties. These are for children "in need", for all looked after children, including those at home, and for all children for whom adoption may be planned. Local authorities and adoption agencies must 'have regard so far as practicable to...[the] child's religious persuasion, racial origin and cultural and linguistic background' when providing services to and in all planning for children who are or may be looked after (s.22(2) and 17(4)(c) of the 1995 Act and s.14(4)(c) of the 2007 Act, as well as both sets of 2009 Regulations). Courts must also take these matters into account in all adoption and permanence order applications (ss.14(4)(c) and 84(5)(b) of the 2007 Act); and in all private law cases (*Osborne v Matthan* 1997 SLT 811, 18 October 1996).

There is no similar statutory provision in the 2011 Act for decisions of children's hearings and courts. However, it must be good legal practice and policy for them to consider these matters, particularly in decisions about compulsory supervision orders and appeals relating to them. Taking these matters into account is implicit in the overarching legal provisions applying and relevant to public authorities: the ECHR, the Equality Act 2010 and the UNCRC. Local authorities must also take these matters into account when planning for and working with children on compulsory supervision orders, s.17(4)(c) of the 1995 Act.

Education issues for Gypsy, Roma and Traveller children in Scotland can be particularly culturally sensitive. Local authorities are responsible for the education of all children in their area under the Education (Scotland) Act 1980 as amended, and every child in Scotland has a right to education, under s.1 of the Standards in Scotland's Schools etc Act 2000. It is crucial for local authorities working with Gypsy, Roma and

Traveller communities to plan co-operatively across all services, to achieve education arrangements that are as flexible and appropriate as possible. Where children wish to continue in education, possibly against the wishes of their communities, they must be supported by all parts of the local authority, in terms of the 1995 Act and all the duties in the education legislation.

Northern Ireland

The Children (Northern Ireland) Order 1995 is the principal statute governing the care, upbringing and protection of children in Northern Ireland, and has implications for all those who work with and care for children, whether parents, paid carers or volunteers. Under Articles 26(2) and (3) of the Children Order 1995, the relevant Health and Social Services Trusts 'must give due regard to those wishes and feelings, having regard to the child's age and understanding, and the child's religious persuasion, racial origin, and cultural and linguistic background'.

The Department of Education is responsible for the education of all children under the Education (Northern Ireland) Order 2006. Taken together with section 75(1) of the Northern Ireland Act 1998, there is a statutory obligation for education providers to promote equality of opportunity. Whilst individual schools are not bound by section 75, the Department of Education and the Education and Library Boards, which finance and govern schools, are. On this basis, education providers in Northern Ireland should recognise the importance of making sure that each Gypsy, Roma and Traveller child and young person is given equal opportunities to access the full curriculum and participate in an inclusive environment in all aspects of school life.

LEGAL SUMMARY

It is important to understand that the legislative frameworks in all four UK countries have shared key elements that impose a range of requirements on local authorities and other public authorities working with Gypsy, Roma and Traveller children, and these cover the work of social work practitioners.

- The views and wishes of Gypsy, Roma and Traveller children should be listened to and acted upon where that is in their best interests.

- Where Gypsy, Roma and Traveller children cannot live with their birth parents, they should be enabled to live with family and friends who, more often than not, will also be from Gypsy, Roma and Traveller communities.

- Wherever they live, Gypsy, Roma and Traveller children have a right to have their culture and ethnicity respected and promoted.

- It is unlawful to discriminate against people on the basis of Gypsy, Roma and Traveller heritage in any area of public life, and services need to be sensitive to the needs of this group.

Human rights and anti-discrimination commissions and related services

This chapter gives some general legal outlines of provisions across the UK, but is not intended as detailed legal advice. Further information may be available from the range of commissions dealing with human rights and anti-discrimination:

- **Equalities and Human Rights Commission (EHRC)** This covers England, Wales and Scotland, and has offices in Cardiff, Glasgow, London and Manchester. Visit www.equalityhumanrights.com/.

- **Equality Advisory Support Service (EASS)** This service has replaced the helpline previously operated by the Equality and Human Rights Commission. The helpline does not provide legal advice but can assist with information in relation to equality matters for those in England, Wales and Scotland. Visit www.equalityadvisoryservice.com/.

- **Scottish Human Rights Commission** Visit www.scottishhumanrights.com/.

- **Equality Commission for Northern Ireland** Visit www.equalityni.org.

- **Northern Ireland Human Rights Commission** Visit www.nihrc.org/.

SOCIAL WORK IN PRACTICE: MISTRUST AND NON-ENGAGEMENT

Although the law requires the state to operate in a way that respects and promotes the heritage of Gypsy, Roma and Traveller children, in practice, the historical oppression of these groups within UK society and the way in which their human rights have been violated (Acton, 1994) sets the context for efforts to apply the law in relation to statutory child care. This raises real questions about how the state can implement laws that require a positive attitude to meeting the ethnic and cultural needs of Gypsy, Roma and Traveller children, while at the same time promoting a social policy that fails to fully protect the human rights of adults and children in those same communities. This is a theme that runs throughout this good practice guide and forms the challenging context in which individual social workers are required to operate.

The corporate parent

The English statutory guidance on *Care Planning, Placement and Case Review* (Department for Education, 2010) sets out the corporate parenting role of local authorities, noting the requirement 'to act as the best possible parent for each child they look after and to advocate on his/her behalf to secure the best possible outcomes'. In an attempt to achieve this in practice, there is an expectation that the corporate parent has a sensitive understanding of the unique needs of each child, and requires that every corporate parent should be as committed to children living in care as they would if they were the actual parent.

However, in applying the idea of corporate parenting to Gypsy, Roma and Traveller children, it soon becomes clear that the concept cannot be meaningfully applied if the corporate parent holds an ideological position that stands in opposition to the interests of that child and the ethnic group to which he or she belongs. The suggestion, therefore, that the corporate parent should support Gypsy, Roma and Traveller children as if they were their own child can become enmeshed within a complex web of contradictions. How can a corporate parent pursue the interests of a particular child, while at the same time being an active part of the state apparatus that discriminates against them, and in part causes the circumstances that result in the child needing to be in care in the first instance?

> In practice, legal requirements to offer services that are accessible by all ethnic groups are often unmet, with inadequate arrangements for accommodation being the norm, and with few if any specialist health or social services to meet the needs of Gypsy, Roma and Traveller people. It is also suggested that the ethnic and cultural needs of Gypsy, Roma and Traveller children in care are too often ignored.

> The consequence of failings in social policy provision is that Gypsy, Roma and Traveller people feel excluded and vulnerable. This is important because its legacy and context have lasting implications in terms of how social care provision in relation to children is perceived and received. Gypsy, Roma and Traveller individuals who have spoken about social work intervention (Allen, 2013) reiterate the need to determine their own private separation from the majority society which can still be seen as a threat to their very existence.

> For this reason, Gypsy, Roma and Traveller communities tend to perceive social work as an interfering agency of social control. Social work practice has been experienced as something being imposed unjustly on the basis that the Gypsy, Roma and Traveller lifestyle is viewed as being incompatible with the best interests of the child. Consequently, this means that there is a considerable lack of contact and trust between social services and Gypsies, Roma and Travellers (Cemlyn, 2000a).

> Since attention from state-sponsored agencies, such as social services, can represent a form of social control that threatens individual,

economic and social freedoms, Allen (2013) explains that it is important to recognise that some families and communities will conceal, or internally regulate, any difficulties they experience in order to protect themselves from this intervention.

NUMBERS OF CHILDREN IN CARE

National statistics regarding the numbers of children living in public care have been maintained in the UK under legislative direction by various inter-governmental organisations since 1969, but in relation to Gypsy, Roma and Traveller children have been of limited value. Until recently, Gypsy, Roma and Traveller children did not fit into the predetermined boxes designated as ethnic groups, and so were labelled as "other". For Richardson (2006), this "othering" has been a specific concern for Gypsy, Roma and Traveller communities and has reflected the lack of importance placed on identifying these specific groups individually or collectively. National statistics on their numbers within the care system have become partially available since 2009 in England and 2010 in Northern Ireland.

Numbers of Gypsy, Roma and Traveller children living in care in England

Ethnicity	2009	2010	2011	2012
Total number of children in care	**60,910**	**64,460**	**65,520**	**67,050**
Travellers of Irish Heritage	30	40	40	50
Gypsy/Roma	30	60	90	120

(Department for Education (2012) *Children Looked After in England (Including Adoption and Care Leavers) Year Ending 31 March 2012*, London: DfE, accessed 8 April 2013, at www.education.gov.uk/rsgateway/DB/SFR/ s001084/sfr20-2012.pdf)

Numbers of Traveller children living in care in Northern Ireland (2011/12)

Ethnicity	Boys	Girls
Total number of children in care	**15,210**	**14,252**
White	7,200	7,009
Refused/unknown	7,581	6,813
Other	291	272
Traveller	63	96
Black	41	26
Chinese	27	23
Indian sub-continent	7	13

(From the Department for Health, Social Services and Public Safety (2012) *Children's Social Care Statistics for Northern Ireland 2011/12,* Stormont: Community Information Branch, accessed 8 April 2013, at www. dhsspsni.gov.uk/children_s_social_care_statistics_for_northern_ireland_2011-12.pdf)

Despite the positive move to include Gypsy, Roma and Traveller children in this data gathering, the formats for doing this fall short of what is required. The issues about the way this information is gathered have the same weaknesses as discussed in relation to data gathering about the community as a whole (see Chapter 2). In Wales and Scotland, such data are not gathered at all.

These limitations notwithstanding, the data from England and Northern Ireland are interesting. In Northern Ireland, Traveller children are the largest defined minority ethnic group, and their numbers could be much greater than indicated, given the huge numbers where information was refused or was not available. In England, recorded numbers are low, but there has been a significant growth over the periods of record-keeping.

This means that we do not know the extent or detail of Gypsy, Roma and Traveller children in public care, but it is highly likely that the current figures significantly underestimate the numbers. It is recognised that Gypsy, Roma and Traveller individuals may often choose not to self-identify, against a background of public hostility to their identity (Cemlyn *et al*, 2009).

Comment from an adoption panel chair

Poppy is a three-year-old child who came to my attention when she was being matched for adoption with her foster carers. Poppy's father was a Gypsy and had been very vocal about this in his relationship with the social worker who had explored whether any of his extended family might look after Poppy, but had concluded that they were unsuitable. Despite this heritage, the reports presented to the panel regarding Poppy described her as a White British child, and her father as White British, only mentioning in passing that he was from a Gypsy background with a history of working on fairgrounds. There was no consideration of how the prospective adopters might meet Poppy's needs arising from her ethnicity.

(Personal correspondence with Paul Adams)

6

Experiences of the care system

There is a dearth of information on the experiences of Gypsy, Roma and Traveller children within the care system, with Allen's (2013) research being the notable exception, consisting of testimonies from 10 Gypsy and Traveller adults who lived in care between the 1970s and 2000s. More specifically, the study sample consisted of eight Irish Travellers, one Gypsy and one Showman, who had each lived in care in either England and/or Ireland, consisting of foster care, residential care and adoption. Where care providers were themselves Gypsies or Travellers, these were in Ireland.

All of the quotations in this chapter come from the participants in Allen's work, using the names given to them in that study to maintain anonymity. They provide a unique and personal perspective on how the care experience affected the participants as children, and subsequently. Although the small scale of Allen's study means that the views of the participants cannot be taken to represent the wider experience of Gypsy and Traveller children in care, this text offers a number of coherent and consistent themes. Some parts of the testimony are emotionally difficult to read, and in this chapter are presented with a minimum of analysis; the stories of these individuals are strong and clear without this.

ON THE EDGE OF CARE

The participants in the study describe how the actions and behaviour of their parents led to their family's isolation and ostracism from their wider Travelling community and also weakened the family structure and supportive systems. In some cases, this led to the intervention of social services.

Testimonies indicate that the collective strength brought about by community cohesion served to ensure the safety and social welfare of its members, but continued membership within this protective system was subject to certain behaviour:

> Laura: You see, in my culture you have to do things a certain way or you'll be ruined. My ma and da were on the drink. My da didn't work and he hit my ma. The others came to our trailer one day and told us to go our own way.

> Interviewer: Why did they tell you to go your own way?

> Laura: Because you are seen as trouble. That you will bring the Travellers a bad name. Now people don't want to be associated with that kind of thing, do they? Life for us Gypsies is hard enough...A lot of what goes on is very hush-hush...but with me da not working and being arrested for hitting our ma, and me ma being arrested for stealing the drink when she should have been minding us, they didn't like that, they seen us as trouble and told us to go off on our own. No one wanted us. OK, it might be your ma and da that are acting up but that doesn't matter, it's family – it's the name.

Where community members behaved in certain ways, they were told to leave, to prevent them from bringing further unwanted attention from state-sponsored agencies. Consistent with this theme, Peter remembered the reaction of his family when his mother decided to move into a women's refuge in order to escape domestic abuse:

> Peter: My mother and father had been into the drink, drugs and raging [fighting] ever since I remember. My mother took us one day to a place for women and children and we stayed there for a few days. I remember my aunty coming in to see her and telling her that she was a disgrace on the family and that no one would want her any more. Me father's friend saw us in the street and spat on us. I suppose that they expected my mother to just deal with the violence and get on with it. She went to that place because she couldn't cope. She would have been dead else but they didn't care. She was his wife and that was the end of it. That was the end for us all.

> Ruth: Some families bring scandal on themselves by fighting, drinking or taking drugs. If this happens the community will turn its back on you. This is when the trouble starts and when the social become involved. Like when a baby animal is separated from the herd, that's when the lions strike.

In order to protect the privacy of the group and avoid the perceived unwanted attention of social workers, these testimonies show that for some it was felt necessary to conceal interfamilial hardships as a measure of self-protection.

With this isolation came a sense of being powerless in the face of social work intervention that discriminated and oppressed rather than supported.

Mary: *The social workers would have said that living on the road was unsuitable.* [Settled] *families are given a house, but my mother and father were only given the choice to put me in a children's home. Because of my disability, my parents were under enormous pressure, they were trying to look after me but they were at the mercy of the system. They were bullied into saying yes. My parents, they wouldn't have questioned why...They couldn't read or write and normally they were sat down and they were blamed [for my disability] because of interfamily marriage. They didn't know that they were able to make a choice; they didn't know that they could say no and to my parents, it was so alien. It was so beyond their culture and reality.*

Helen: [During a home visit] *I remember begging them* [her parents] *please, please, please, don't send me back [to the children's home], and again through their own naivety they didn't think that we could come out. They thought they had to wait until we were released.*

COMING INTO CARE

Although those people who describe coming into care provide unique testimonies, the accounts have strong similarities and connections with each other. For most, the memories associated with the hours leading up to their accommodation were happy ones because instead of being told that they would be leaving home to move into care, they were made to feel special and loved by the increased attention and positive treatment that they experienced from their parents.

Mary: *My parents told me that I would be going on to a special school for people with disabilities...I was happy at first because I remember getting a lot more attention than normal...The day before I went, I remember my mother and her friends washing me and getting me ready. I had a walking frame and a new little pink dress. My mother had no money to buy things but she had still managed to buy me a new dress. They all fussed over me....It was as if I was the most important person in the world. I felt loved...*

Helen: *We were led to believe that we were going on holiday. A special mini-break. It was arranged through the Catholic school and we were told to keep it a secret...The day before, I remember spending the whole day with my mam packing my bag. I was given new underwear and vests and my da gave me some pocket money. In the morning, I remember having a fry* [cooked breakfast] *and the holiday men coming for us in their fancy car. I went with my sister and my brother and we were taken from our parents' trailer, kind of excited but kind of frightened as well. I had never been away from my parents before. I felt good though – really important – I thought to myself the others* [children] *would be dead jealous if they could see me.*

Peter: *The mother was like a new person. She started to love us and that and tell us stories and sing us songs at night. My brother said she had gone mad in the head with all the drink but I remember feeling like a child again. It's strange because I was eight, but I missed that. I suppose I wanted it to stay like that forever...*

The description of feeling special and loved is crucial to understanding the way in which the people who took part in this study were prepared, or not, for the experience of going into care. At times, it was almost as if their parents' actions spoke louder than words, or expressed things that words could not.

Ruth: *A few hours after the social left, my father called us into the trailer for supper. I should have realised something was going on then and I went inside and Ma was sitting at the table with a big fruitcake that I think she had made. I sat down and they gave us a big slice of cake and I thought that it was great and we sat in silence and Da made some tea and* Catchphrase *was on the telly. My ma had tears in her eyes...She told us that she loved us and that she always would, and she told us a story about a magic fiddle and got us all to sing to her and promise that we would always look after one another. We never really did anything like that, you know, and I remember thinking that something...I suppose I thought we were having a treat. We only did things like that on special occasions...I didn't think the cake was for us.* [Sobbing] *I didn't think that it was going to be our last supper. I wouldn't have eaten it otherwise.*

However, these positive feelings were quickly replaced by feelings of shock and trauma as the children began to realise the reality of their situation.

Helen: *At first, we thought it was the holiday people coming to collect us but it turned out to be social workers and instead of going on holiday like me mammy had said, we were going in care...I remember them coming for us in their fancy car. I went with my sister and my brother and we were taken from our parents' trailer. And then as soon as they got us in the car, they were shouting at us to shut up and stop making a noise. You know, stop the crying and the tears...We were devastated, betrayed and humiliated. I will never forget that feeling as long as I live.*

For most of the people who described their experiences, the actual event of being taken into care, and the lack of preparation for it, was hugely distressing.

Ruth: *I remember the police coming with the social and knocking on the door and my ma flying out and screaming and shouting and I didn't know what was happening. And I got my sister and ran out and saw Ma hitting the police so I did it too and they tried to lock my ma in the van and put me and my sister in the car and came out of the trailer with our things in black bin bags and I wanted to fight and get my ma, the woman [social worker] was telling us to calm down, I scratched her face and she called me wild, the car drove off, and the police were left fighting with me ma. I didn't know that that was the last day I would see my ma... the memory is making me feel sick...I can't get it out of my mind...I dream about it, you know.* [Sobbing] *Me ma loved us but she couldn't mind us.*

However, for some people their entry into care came as a welcome form of protection from their exposure to violence and abuse at home. This was true in Michael's case, even though he was placed with foster carers from the majority community:

Michael: *It was happy, I think, pleasant. Different surroundings, change of scenery, you know, there wasn't fighting and arguing, there wasn't drink, you know, but the carers were just ordinary happy people...I suppose at the time that was the surroundings I wanted to be in, I didn't want the whole, er, the fighting, the drink, you know, all that side of things...I felt kind of loved, you felt loved, probably for the first time in a long time, you know, there was peace of mind, you know, different surroundings, different life.*

FEELING DIFFERENT: RACISM AND ABUSE

For the majority of people who took part in Allen's (2013) study, the process of moving into care represented the loss of a Traveller and Gypsy identity, including being made to feel different, often through racist abuse by carers and others. As children, they remember feeling cut off from family and community, and immersed in an alien culture that attempted to assimilate them:

Mary: *I was pushed into a bath and scrubbed because they told me I was dirty because I was from a Traveller family. I had beautifully thick, long black hair; if you stood me in a line with the other girls, you could tell that I was a Traveller because of my hair. The care workers cut it all off...because they said it was dirty...they threw my pink dress away and gave me some other clothes to wear...They made you feel like they were doing you a favour, and that they were saving you from an awful life because you were a Traveller.*

Ruth: *The first memory I have of the foster home was how closed in it was. The house was dark and smelt of damp... there were stairs...I'd never seen stairs. I remember my bedroom being next to the toilet...I remember thinking to myself how dirty that was. It wasn't anything that I was used to...It was like unlearning what I knew was right... unlearning the Traveller way of life. The foster woman cried when she saw me and told me to get into the bath. She took my clothes and told me that she was going to throw them in the bin. They were the only things that I had. She gave me a pair of jogging bottoms and a T-shirt of the other girl that lived there...I suppose to her I must have looked different, but to me they were trying to wash away my Traveller identity.*

Ruth: *You trust these people to look after children but they hated us, especially the foster carers. They hated our culture. In the Traveller culture, girls get their ears pierced at about three weeks old. They didn't understand the culture, they wanted to change it. You were an innocent child who didn't know what was going on and you were persecuted for having a culture. You have to accept who people are and where they come from. You can't try and change people – it is wrong.*

Helen: *The people who was running it. They treated us completely different to the other children. It was almost, like, looking at it from a child's point of view, that they didn't like us. They had made their minds up before we had even got there and I believe that was because we were Travellers. They were just horrible to us. We had to go to bed at, like, six o'clock and the other children were allowed to play downstairs...We all had to bathe together with boys and girls. I mean, I had never seen boy's bits before and although we had a brother, we never saw, you know, bits! We just weren't used to that, you know, coming from a Travelling family. We all washed separately, you know, so it was like a culture shock for me to have to go through this. You were frightened to cry because you got punished and thrown upstairs in the bedroom.*

In some cases, people described racist bullying and abuse from the adults or other children and young people.

Mary: [Sobbing] [It was] *Humiliating, degrading, disgusting, lonely, isolated. You feel your life was nothing; you were nothing...They used to beat us...They became random acts of violent racism, physical violence, sexual violence, emotional and psychological violence. They thought they could beat our ethnicity and cultural identity out of us.*

Peter: *One night, the other boys in the home got into my bedroom and pulled me out of bed. They had been drinking and poured beer on me and pissed on me. They squirted my toiletries at me and called me filthy pikey. They barricaded the door and set about beating me, saying that I would fight back if I was a proper Gypsy.*

For these people, the experience of coping with racism meant a combination of trying to maintain cultural norms in the face of attack, and minimising or playing down their Gypsy and Traveller culture, effectively internalising the racism. Ruth describes this very clearly:

Ruth: *When other Traveller children came, even when you would gravitate towards them, an emotional and psychological gravitation, particularly if they were younger children, you would want to mind [look after] them, you know?...It was like I wasn't alone. In my culture there are women like matrons, who don't have their own children but mind other people's children. I was like that. I felt important because those children needed me and I needed them. I looked out for them. I was, like, what I was meant to do. It made me feel good.*

Ruth: *I remember crying and crying and my sister getting into my bed to give me a cuddle before the foster carer came in and threw her out and called us dirty. We were not dirty; you have to bear in mind we were used to sleeping together in trailers. To me it was normal, but I was*

> *embarrassed, they made me feel dirty...Like I needed to wash away my Gypsy ways. Like I was not normal...It was like they hated us and I could feel it on my skin.*

Ruth: *The kids at my new school picked on me because of my accent...I told my foster family but they didn't care...So I thought, oh well, I won't speak with an accent any more; that way, no one will know I am a Traveller. I wanted to make the Traveller me invisible...but it didn't work. The kids carried on picking on me anyway, saying I was just trying to be like them.*

Peter also tried downplaying his cultural heritage, but when this was ineffective, in the end he had to fight back:

Interviewer: *What did the care staff do [about the bullying]?*

Peter: *Nothing. They said that I could phone the police. From that moment I just kept myself to myself. I had to change. I thought that they...that they would somehow leave me alone if I was quiet.*

Interviewer: *Did it work?*

Peter: [Laughing] *Did it fuck! Over time, I started dealing them the drugs and selling them the alcohol. A year or so later I got the lad that pissed all on me and broke his head with a brick. They sent me to secure for that one, but no one bothered me again. You see, quiet didn't work on its own... do you know what I mean?*

Mary had the opportunity to escape abuse in a residential setting by being fostered by families from the majority community, but made sense of this as a further attempt by this community to take away her Traveller identity:

Mary: *I remember one family that I could have lived with buying me a large doll's house. All the other children were jealous of me because they said the doll's house was so beautiful and the carers told me that I was very lucky to have such a wonderful foster family, but I smashed it up. I smashed it up and no one could understand why. But I know why. I never wanted to live in a house, I never wanted a doll's house, I never wanted to be settled, I never wanted to be like them, the idea of that was alien to me. They were trying to take away my Traveller identity. But they weren't able to. They weren't able to.*

RELATIONSHIP WITH FAMILY AND COMMUNITY

Although, for some people, responsibility for the absence of contact was placed firmly with neglectful and uninterested parents, for others the blame lay elsewhere. The practical arrangements were often culturally insensitive, and failed to take into consideration the fact that many Traveller and Gypsy families may not have a permanent address or even access to a telephone. This had a significant impact when family visiting was scheduled for specific times and days:

Mary: *Number one: my parents were not able to read or write so they could not read the letters that the institute sent them. Number two: they lived on the roadside so they did not have a permanent address. I wasn't able to write them a letter. Number three: they were on the road with their own children. They had no money to drive to see me and when they would come [to visit me] it might be on the wrong day, or the wrong time. [Sobbing] They might have driven hundreds of miles to see me and when they arrived the staff turned them away when they got there because they had arrived on the wrong day, and they would not see me. I remember crying as I could see them out of my window and hear the staff telling them to leave.*

Even where contact did take place, this was difficult where the children's day-to-day care experiences would bring their values and rituals into conflict with their birth family and community. Although Mary quite obviously resisted assimilation, she was aware that her environment was making it difficult for her to have meaningful contact with her family and community:

Mary: *When I was around other Travellers, I knew I was different. I had the smell of the institution on me. I was losing my accent. I wasn't allowed to wear Traveller clothes any more and I was losing my Traveller culture and identity... You didn't understand when you went home. You didn't know your family. You had to relearn the Traveller stuff. I was bringing home certain settled values and then was making a fool of myself in front of my family.*

With the exception of the four people in the study placed with Traveller foster carers, for those leaving care the opportunity to reintegrate to the Traveller or Gypsy community was made that much harder because they were seen by some community members as being non-Travellers or Gypsies. For these people, there was a growing sense that they did not fit into the settled community because they wanted to maintain their Traveller or Gypsy identity. However, at the same time, they also felt that they did not fit within the Traveller or Gypsy community, because they did not belong to that group either.

> Josephine: *Because I felt that I have been sheltered from the Showmen world, I bought a trailer and took to the road to look for my parents, but the community didn't want me and the social took my children into care and now they live with settled people and they will never know the Traveller way...*

This constituted a double blow: stigmatised by the care system due to cultural differences, and stigmatised by the way in which the Travelling community can stigmatise those who have lived in care. This was particularly the case for women:

> Ruth: *When I left care, I tried to get back in with my family. My uncle and aunty took me on and let me live in their trailer for a while. When we went to fairs and that, all the boys would all look down at me and call me dirty. They knew that I had been in care and they all thought that I was like a settled girl. That I had been having sex, that I had been to nightclubs and that I had taken drugs. You see, the country [settled] people look at us and see what they think are Gypsies. The same way boys look at me and see a settled girl. Because what they have seen on the television, and that they think that I am dirty, and because of this, no man in his right mind would marry me. If someone did, they would be outcast.*

> Helen: *If people knew that I had been in care, they would think that I had been going on like a settled girl, going clubbing, drinking, taking drugs, and having sex. They would think that I was dirty and that I had lost the Traveller way. People would say that I was half radge* [settled, not a real Traveller]. *Nobody wants to talk with someone that is half radge...I never did those things. It's not my fault I was sent into care.*

SECRECY AND STIGMA

Because of this stigma, it is normal for Gypsy and Traveller women in particular to be unable to tell others about having been in care.

> Helen: *I haven't told anybody* [about living in care]. *There is only my parents and brother and sister that know. Because of domestic violence, we were classed as social outcasts and none of our family knew that we were taken into care. I wouldn't tell anybody.* [If people found out] *you'd be*

shunned. They would think you were half radge [settled, not a real Traveller], *they would think that there was something wrong with ya. My aunties and uncles and cousins don't even know that we went into care.*

For some women, even their husbands did not know about their care history, and Laura was asked about why this was:

Laura: *Because he would leave me.*

Interviewer: *Why would he leave you?*

Laura: *Because he'd see me as dirty. I have to hide all of that. It's a secret. I can't talk about it because I would be humiliated.*

Interviewer: *Is it easy to keep it a secret?*

Laura: *Ah Jesus!* [Shouting] *Is it easy to live a lie? Is it easy to hide it all? Is it easy to be someone I am not?* [Talking] *What do you think?*

Whilst three people who took part in this study described being socially accepted within the community because of the fact that they had managed to keep their history secret, they all explained that the pressures of hiding the truth had a serious impact on their emotional well-being. Helen's account reflects the emotional cost of maintaining the secrecy:

Helen: *I actually had a mental breakdown a few years ago and that's when I decided to talk about it with my family and my counsellor. You can't have a breakdown in the Traveller community because you'd be looked upon like you were half radge. Again, you bring humiliation to your family. You'd be ruined....No one knows about my breakdown. I was in hospital and they thought I went off with the trailer for a few months.*

Travellers and Gypsies remain silenced by their experiences because of the social humiliation that the disclosures of being in care could bring. This secrecy and stigma militates against discussion of the issues of being in care, and contributes to the marginalisation of Travellers and Gypsies within the care system.

7

Anti-discriminatory casework

Previous chapters make clear that working with Gypsy, Roma and Traveller children and families is inevitably going to be complex and challenging, taking place as it does in a context of conflict and disregard for human rights. A casework approach that does not recognise this context is destined to be ineffective, and this chapter argues in favour of an anti-discriminatory approach (Thompson, 2006) influenced by radical social work theory (Bailey and Brake, 1980). Although not set out in quite the same terms as these, it is also important to note that the social work regulatory bodies within the UK require social workers to take account of equality and diversity within their work, and this very much applies in relation to Gypsy, Roma and Traveller children and families.

Health and Care Professions Council: Standards of Proficiency – Social Workers in England (2012)

5.   Be aware of the impact of culture, equality and diversity on practice.

5.1   Be able to reflect on and take account of the impact of inequality, disadvantage and discrimination on those who use social work services and their communities.

5.2   Understand the need to adapt practice to respond appropriately to different groups and individuals.

5.3   Be aware of the impact of their own values on practice with different groups of service users and carers.

5.4   Understand the impact of different cultures and communities and how this affects the role of the social worker in supporting service users and carers.

ENGAGING GYPSY, ROMA AND TRAVELLER FAMILIES

For social workers attempting to support Gypsy, Roma and Traveller children living in the community or entering care, engagement is likely to be in an environment characterised by tension and community resentment. Gypsy, Roma and Traveller families and communities will likely be of the view that social work involvement is a threat to their privacy and right to private life, and will be seen as part of the state oppression that characterises Gypsy, Roma and Traveller experience. This demands a particular approach from the allocated social worker to the family.

Good practice in engaging Gypsy, Roma and Traveller families

- Reflect on your own attitudes and values, and avoid assumptions.

- Acknowledge the context of your involvement.

- Be clear about the specific child-related concerns and what needs to change.

- Listen, engage and form relationships.

- Help families and communities understand social work processes.

- Understand cultural aspects of communication.

Reflect on your own attitudes and values, and avoid assumptions

As a social worker, it is important that you understand what you are bringing to the relationship in terms of attitudes and beliefs, and to what extent these simply reflect societal stereotypes and the dominant view. This is discussed at length in this chapter, but good practice demands specific efforts to isolate any presuppositions about Gypsy, Roma and Traveller children, families, and communities, and to consider how these may influence professional judgements and undermine the legitimacy of an assessment.

Acknowledge the context of your involvement

From the outset it is important that you acknowledge that your relationship with Gypsy, Roma and Traveller children, families and communities is fixed within the historical, social, and political dynamics which have served to construct certain boundary distinctions between Gypsy, Roma and Traveller and majority communities.

As a result, relationships between social workers and Gypsy, Roma and Traveller families will, at least initially, probably be characterised by suspicion and fear (Cemlyn et al, 2009), and this can only be dealt with if it is first acknowledged. In line with Ferguson (2011), this might necessitate comments like:

- I appreciate that you do not want me to interfere in your life. It must be very hard for you to accept me being involved in your family, given that you do not like it.

And later move on to dialogue such as:

- It is very important that I work with you and your family. How can we work together in a productive way so that I do not need to be involved in your family any more?

Be clear about specific child-related concerns and what needs to change

Linked to this, it must be made obvious that social work involvement is not being instigated with the Gypsy, Roma or Traveller family on the grounds that they are from a particular ethnic and cultural group, but more accurately because there are real and tangible concerns about their child's welfare. As a social worker, it is important that you are very clear about this, emphasising that the welfare of the child is paramount. Families will need to understand that where there is criticism of them, this relates to the impact of their parenting on the child, and is not a criticism of their culture or community lifestyle.

Social workers should make clear that any formal child protection processes, including court action, will only be used if the family show, or have shown, that they are unable to protect the child from harm. It is equally important to be clear about what needs to change in order for the local authority to be less concerned and be able to reduce or change the focus of their intervention.

Listen, engage and form relationships

To avoid applying presuppositions or preconceived ideas, you will need instead to gain understanding from engaging with and listening to the family's own reported experience. This dialogue offers an opportunity to communicate a sense of genuine interest and a determination to form an alliance in working together to achieve mutually satisfactory solutions. This might involve asking questions such as:

- How do you define yourself and what words do you use?

- What does being a Gypsy/Roma/Traveller mean to you?

- What are the main differences between your culture and the majority culture?

- What does the experience of living on a campsite/by the roadside/in a house mean to you as a Gypsy, Roma and Traveller?

- What is a typical day like for you?

- In what way do your family and community support you?

- What is the hardest thing about being a Gypsy, Roma or Traveller?

- If you could change three things about your current situation, what would you change?

By asking questions such as these, the family's own understanding of what it means to be Gypsy, Roma and Traveller can be explored. This process is also likely to establish a picture of Gypsy, Roma and Traveller culture in relation to the specific family in question, what being Gypsy, Roma and Traveller means in their lived experience; what the practical and emotional features of being Gypsy, Roma and Traveller entail. Although you may believe that you know some of the answers, the questions serve to communicate clear messages to the family that no judgements are being made about their unique lives and cultural mores. This is likely to engender a sense of trust and start to provide more clarity about the present situation.

By taking this approach, the most important factor is to allow children, families, groups and communities the time to talk about the challenges that they experience, because information gathered from these responses can be used to develop a deeper, more meaningful and accurate assessment of the family's situation. In particular, it allows opportunities to talk about experiences of racist harassment, enforced eviction, and any issues in accessing education, health and social care services. It will also assist families to talk openly and candidly about their concerns regarding the impact of social work attention, and how they might be perceived for having brought this scrutiny into their community.

Case example: a respectful approach to working together

I have worked with a number of Gypsy, Roma and Traveller families, and engaging and developing an honest and real relationship is crucial. I have found that asking questions is good, but that taking responsibility for my own learning is important too. The families are not there to teach me, but have appreciated my positivity and interest about their community.

I have learnt with one carer, through honest dialogue, that there are some important and significant family events (weddings, funerals, baptisms, etc) when the family will have many visitors to the household. She has stressed that on these occasions she would prefer not to have a social worker visiting or calling, unless it is really urgent. Some social workers have expectations that they can phone or visit whenever they need or suits them, and if families are uncomfortable with that it is seen as non-cooperation.

However, I have developed a strategy whereby the carer will inform me in advance if an event is to take place and I will try to be flexible where possible. I am mindful that many community members are uncomfortable with social workers, and if this carer is seen as being too close to us then that makes things difficult for her. The thing is that she is firmly rooted in her community and this is a real positive aspect of her care of the children. Social workers need to understand and respect this, and adapt their practice appropriately.

(Personal communication with Paul Adams)

Help families and communities understand social work processes

Gypsy, Roma and Traveller families, like many others who come into contact with statutory services, are unlikely to understand the various social work processes. If any assessment is being undertaken, it is crucial that families understand what this entails, what is being judged, and what changes are necessary to reduce concerns. If there is to be a child protection conference, then the family will need to understand how this works in order to prepare and participate to the best of their ability. Where appropriate, a family group conference could also be used (see later in this chapter).

None of this is different to any other family, but the situation might feel particularly alien to members of Gypsy, Roma and Traveller communities if they have had very little contact with formal government structures, and in any case feel under threat from them. In this context, it is particularly important that families have information about their rights including sources of independent support and the relevant complaints procedures. However, at the same time as working effectively with families, good practice demands that the child is placed at the centre of the social work intervention.

Understand cultural aspects of communication

Asking generalised or hypothetical questions such as those proposed earlier in this chapter can create an opportunity to reduce conflict and lessen the likelihood of attempts to undermine social work involvement by transferring the power, or expertise in problem resolution, to the family. As a useful method in the social work assessment, this style of questioning can prove invaluable when applied strategically in carefully considered conversation.

However, using generalised or hypothetical questions as a strategy in assessment raises some concerns regarding the need to exercise a degree of sensitivity to cultural and social mores. Some Gypsies, Roma and Travellers may perceive such questions with suspicion as they require a degree of social or emotional imagination that may otherwise be seen as unusual, and some people may respond by protecting against or circumnavigating the topic being discussed. Meaningful attempts should also be made to verify responses through more direct and deliberate forms of inquiry. This approach should always focus on lived experience and engage children, families and communities so as to allow them to discuss their strengths, weaknesses, opportunities and threats. In this sense, social workers may be in a stronger position to help families and communities understand social work processes better, and demonstrate that intervention can be more equal, inclusive and based on respect.

As well as being aware of the impact of verbal communication, you should also be critically aware of social presentation. For some families, the formal appearance of some social workers in smart office wear could be perceived as intimidating and threatening. If a social worker were to enter some sites formally dressed, they may raise serious suspicions within the community as to why they are visiting a particular person. Such attire may also serve to emphasise differences in power and culture, so it is suggested that some thought is given to the need to recognise how external impressions are likely to impact on forming relationships.

Case example: working with Roma families

In my work for the Roma Support Group, I have been involved in a number of cases where Roma families were involved with social workers. In our work, we noticed that language can create huge barriers in engagement between Roma and social workers. Social services frequently need to use interpreting services in order to communicate. On most occasions, an interpreter speaking one of the Romany dialects is not available so the only choice is to use an interpreter who speaks the language spoken in the country the family came from. Usually it is a second language for Roma and often their vocabulary in this language is limited. An additional barrier to communication can be that many Roma would not only have problems understanding words but also whole concepts. It is really important that social workers understand that some social work words do not easily translate into Romany or other languages used by Roma. For example, I was supporting one Roma family who were struggling with the care of their child, and the social worker asked them if they thought that they would benefit from parenting classes. But once the interpreter had translated this, the family thought the social worker was offering them sex education. The family were deeply embarrassed and told the social worker no. As a result, it appeared that the family was reluctant to co-operate with the social worker. Luckily, the social worker had the insight to check with the parents what they thought parenting classes were. Once this had been clarified, the family was happy and grateful for the opportunity to learn how to look after their child. The meaning of words, particularly social work terms, is so important when working with Roma. They may never have heard about things like parenting classes before.

(Personal communication with Daniel Allen)

The Roma Support Group is a Roma-led charity working with East European Roma refugees and migrants. Since 1998, they have worked with thousands of Roma families, offering them a variety of services and ensuring that the safeguarding needs of Roma children are met. They have also supported professionals, including social workers, working with the Roma across the UK through expert advice, crisis interventions and training. For more information, see Useful Organisations.

A CHILDREN'S RIGHTS APPROACH

Safe practice

Safe and competent social work practice emphasises that the child must be seen as the priority for the social worker. This not only complies with the UN Convention on the Rights of the Child (1989), which sees the child as an individual with rights, but fits comfortably with an anti-discriminatory approach that understands the need for social workers to take the side of the most vulnerable.

As a social worker, you should be prepared to recognise the complexity and moral dilemmas at the heart of social work practice with all marginalised groups, and you should also be clear that a duty to safeguard and protect the welfare of children is the driving responsibility. As shown in Lord Laming's report (2003), reticence regarding social work involvement on the grounds of cultural sensitivity – the fear of being accused of racism – undermines professionalism and the function of statutory intervention.

So while it is important to understand the concern that formal social work involvement might result in social rejection and shame for some in the Gypsy, Roma and Traveller community, it is also vital not to compromise your involvement on this basis, or fall into practice described in the "rule of optimism".

The rule of optimism

It is generally accepted that social workers want to make a positive difference to the lives of the people they work with, and they want to believe that their interventions are effective. However, excessive optimism can lead to unsafe practice, particularly when it is combined with a disproportionate desire to not be seen as discriminating against a vulnerable group of people. This unsafe practice can include:

● believing that a family's situation is "culturally" acceptable;

● having unrealistic expectations of individuals, families and communities;

● anticipating and assuming the effectiveness of social work intervention;

● focusing only on strengths and offering overly positive interpretations of what is happening;

● filtering out or minimising areas of real concern and the risks that arise from them;

● apologising, or allowing oneself to be made to feel guilty for social work involvement.

The rule of optimism reminds social work practitioners about the need for a balanced and objective assessment that recognises progress and achievements, but always keeps risk in mind. This requires practice which is critically reflective, and which makes good use of supervisory processes.

(Dingwall *et al*, 1983)

Listening to children

A children's rights approach also requires social workers to fully engage with and listen to Gypsy, Roma and Traveller children and to hear their views, wishes, hopes and aspirations. You should also recognise that listening requires sensitivity to the fact that Gypsy, Roma and Traveller children, in particular, might be feeling confused, powerless and vulnerable, struggling to share their real concerns without being disloyal to their family and community. This is an issue for all children involved with statutory social work services, but is particularly acute for children from marginalised and oppressed groups. Failing to recognise this creates a significant barrier to effective communication and potentially risks silencing the voices of Gypsy, Roma and Traveller children who might be experiencing severe trauma.

While effective communication with Gypsy, Roma and Traveller children can be a major factor in achieving good improved outcomes, a lack of empathy and trust in the social worker can lead Gypsy, Roma and Traveller children to feel alienated from the decisions that are being made about them. Where they are placed with carers from the majority community, children can find themselves being left to make sense of their experiences on their own. For Gypsy, Roma and Traveller children who do not receive appropriate support, the shock of moving into care is characterised by the lack of opportunity to participate in this new context as they encounter insecurity, fear and social rejection.

In considering these issues of communication, it is important to recognise that some children brought up in the context of strong boundary separations between Gypsy, Roma and Traveller people and the majority community may remain determined to keep certain matters private from those they perceive as "outsiders". For this reason, social workers should be aware that some Gypsy, Roma and Traveller children may choose not to talk to outsiders about themselves or their families, particularly when those outsiders represent state agencies that are perceived to be oppressive. Instead, the child's right to participate may require specific arrangements involving other Gypsy, Roma and Traveller community members, although this may be difficult to achieve.

Support and empowerment

In situations where ongoing social work help is required, care should be taken to identify appropriate methods of support which can account for the unique needs of the child and family being supported. This means asking families what they want or think they need to improve their situation, and ultimately move to a position of independence where social work involvement is no longer required. This encourages families to exercise power and take ownership of plans, empowering them to realise and make use of their own opportunities and strengths.

The ability of social workers to communicate in ways such as this can prove to be a useful strategy in reducing conflict and the possibility that individuals will attempt to undermine social work involvement. By engaging children, families and communities so to allow them to discuss their strengths, weaknesses, opportunities and threats, social work can begin to challenge the Gypsy, Roma and Traveller/majority community distinction, and begin moving towards a relationship based on mutual respect. Not only will this square with the responsibility to challenge inequality, but it may also enable practice to constructively align to the principles of advocacy explored below.

Family group conferences

A family group conference (FGC) is a decision-making and planning forum in which the wider family group makes plans and decisions for children and young people who have been identified, either by the family themselves or by service providers, as being in need of a plan that will safeguard and promote their welfare. The child is directly involved in the process, and the family plan that is devised must take account of any stipulations made by the referring agency (typically the local authority) for it to be agreed.

FGCs should be considered as an effective method of engaging the support of wider family and friends at the early stage of concerns about a child who may not be able to live with their parents. They promote the involvement of the wider family in the decision-making process to achieve a resolution of difficulties, and offer a way of ensuring that all resources within the family's wider social networks have been engaged for the benefit of the child.

(Department for Education, 2011)

The existence of fear and mistrust between social workers and minority groups is not a new phenomenon, and commentators such as Cemlyn (2000a) and Thompson (2006) highlight the need for social work agencies to utilise theories of community engagement and to forge effective links with the communities they seek to support. Effectively supporting Gypsy, Roma and Traveller families might typically involve putting them in touch with, and working in partnership with, other organisations, including Gypsy, Roma and Traveller community organisations, details of which are listed at the end of this guide.

Haringey Travelling People's Team

Turning suspicion into trust is never easy, and in Haringey this has been attempted by setting up a small specialist team to work with the estimated 2,500 Gypsies, Roma and Travellers living in the borough. The team delivers a model that attempts to engage the community by offering positive and valuable services.

One successful example has been a driving theory support group for younger Travellers, addressing the fact that the written component of driving tests is often a difficult hurdle for a largely illiterate community that highly values the freedom to travel. Another example is a football club for younger members that also runs a drop-in centre, offers job-training workshops and has fostered strong relationships with partners in education and training.

Advocacy

As discussed throughout this guide, Gypsy, Roma and Traveller communities face discrimination from state organisations, and anti-discriminatory social work practice advocates the need to identify and challenge such inequality. In practice, this requires individual social workers to advocate for Gypsy, Roma and Traveller families with various service providers, including with their own local authority. Concerns about the safe care of children do not arise in isolation, and where local authority service provision is failing to meet the needs of Gypsy, Roma and Traveller families, then they are contributing to the difficulties and discriminating against this group of children. An anti-oppressive social work perspective requires that the social worker does not collude with this, but challenges such an approach, thereby advocating for Gypsy, Roma and Traveller children.

This might include highlighting how the local authority is failing to provide appropriate accommodation either because of providing poor quality sites or by evicting Gypsy, Roma and Traveller families, or forcing them into bricks-and-mortar housing that leaves them feeling depressed and isolated (Parry et al, 2004). Similarly, where appropriate and relevant, social workers should challenge the local authority about failures to offer culturally sensitive services in education, health, mental health, domestic violence, alcohol, and substance misuse. Where these factors are contributing to poor standards of parenting, social workers should make this link, showing that the difficulties and risks being experienced by the child are directly linked to inadequate services and wider failures in accommodation and social care provision.

Working both "for" and "with" Gypsy, Roma and Traveller communities requires social workers to challenge the status quo and be proactive in the development of policy and practice that recognise the impact of oppression and discrimination. Where social workers choose to highlight structural inequality in this way, they can also begin to challenge the idea that social work practice is inevitably on behalf of an oppressive agency, which serves to limit economic and cultural freedoms. By proving that local authorities are ready to work with Gypsy, Roma and Traveller families and communities in matters of social justice as well as family support and protection, practitioners can begin to reverse certain Gypsy, Roma and Traveller/majority community distinctions, and instead promote the core social work traditions of understanding, partnership and meaningful support.

8
Promoting cultural competence

However effectively social workers engage in anti-discriminatory casework with Gypsy, Roma and Traveller children and their families, there will always be some cases where this is not enough to keep children safe, and they will need to come into state care. For these Gypsy, Roma and Traveller children, it is essential that social workers, foster carers and others are able to promote culturally competent practice.

Vonk (2001) offers a helpful framework for considering the importance of promoting cultural competence:

> It is not enough to be aware of how race and culture affect self-functioning; individuals also must be open to learning about the effect of race and culture on others, to learning about racism and mechanisms of oppression, and to acquiring the cross-cultural skills that enable effective intervention.

For Vonk, there are three specific aspects that make up cultural competence:

- racial awareness;
- multicultural planning; and
- promoting survival skills for children who will need to learn to deal with racism.

The following discussion looks at these issues as they pertain to working with or caring for Gypsy, Roma and Traveller children, and assumes that social workers, foster carers and others working with a child will usually come from a majority community background. This discussion is very much in line with the recommendations presented by Cemlyn (2000a; 2000b), Fisher (2003) and Allen (2012; 2013) in relation to effective social work practice with Gypsy and Traveller children.

RACIAL AWARENESS

Social workers report that they can feel anxious about their ability to work effectively with Gypsy, Roma and Traveller communities (Power, 2004). Confronted with their own "culture shock", they can perceive caravans, trailers, outhouses, and the often run-down utility blocks, high fences, and cramped layout in a way that reinforces racist perceptions and fear. If social workers can feel out of place while visiting a campsite, their subjective value judgements can influence their assessment of risk, and be used to justify the need for formal social work involvement. By contrast, good anti-discriminatory practice will depend on an informed understanding of the unique challenges faced by Gypsy, Roma and Traveller children and families in society.

Racial self-awareness is crucial in relation to working with Gypsy, Roma and Traveller children living in state care, and applies equally to foster carers, residential workers and others as it does to social workers. Working effectively with Gypsy, Roma and Traveller children is not a question of treating them in exactly the same way as might be appropriate where the carer shares the same ethnic background, but rather is about recognising that a child who has a different background and culture to that of the carer will require specific measures to be taken in order to meet *all* of the child's needs, including their cultural needs. The first step in being able to offer this is for the social worker and the foster carer or residential worker to be able to reflect on their own understanding of Gypsy, Roma and Traveller cultures, and evaluate how their personal views about Gypsy, Roma and Traveller people could influence the care that they provide.

The realisation of culturally competent care for children from Gypsy, Roma and Traveller communities remains problematic for a number of reasons. Most obviously, Gypsy, Roma and Traveller children often look similar to children from the majority community and so it is easy to ignore real difference. Also, because many important aspects of Gypsy, Roma and Traveller culture are passed on orally from generation to generation and not written down, social workers and carers might find it difficult to recognise and understand significant and important cultural practices.

Nevertheless, Gypsy, Roma and Traveller children who are placed with carers from the majority community are living in a cultural environment that is different from their own. Many Gypsy, Roma and Traveller children have the experience of having to make sense of different social mores and social conventions, and learn to come to terms with the fact that their carers generally view the world differently to their Gypsy, Roma and Traveller families and communities. This can be extremely stressful (Lau and Ridge, 2011), and if there is no opportunity to reflect on this with people they trust and who are also reflecting on these

Local sources of information and learning

Several techniques can be employed to enhance relationships with Gypsy, Roma and Traveller communities. These might include those listed below.

- **Liaise with the Traveller Education Support Service**

Most local education authorities organise specific Traveller Education Support Services that aim to help Gypsy, Roma and Traveller parents find places in local schools for their children. The Traveller Education Support Service also supports schools by offering advice, teaching support and home/school links so that they can meet the needs of Gypsy, Roma and Traveller pupils who may be home tutored. In terms of social work practice, the Traveller Education Support Service could also work with social work departments and other agencies to raise awareness of Traveller culture and help address prejudiced views.

- **Liaise with Gypsy, Roma and Traveller liaison officers**

A number of local authorities employ Gypsy and Traveller liaison officers to manage residential and transit sites. They are responsible for assisting families who are camping on unauthorised sites and work closely with police and the Traveller Education Support Service when undertaking welfare enquiries. In most cases, the liaison officer may personally know the families living within the local area, and for this reason, they might be able to provide key information about culture, family difficulties, health, education, and so forth. In some cases, the Gypsy and Traveller liaison officer might also offer assistance and advice when planning initial contact.

- **Develop relationships with Gypsy, Roma and Traveller communities**

The need to develop links and community relations is an essential component in the achievement of proactive and preventative support. Whilst social work is becoming increasingly driven by crisis intervention, social work teams must consider how they could engage Gypsy, Roma and Traveller communities in a more meaningful and focused way, to address difficulties at an early stage and before they become crises.

- **Keep a resource file in the office**

The opportunity to develop relationships with Gypsies, Roma and Travellers can be enhanced by a social worker who has a sensitive and considered understanding of cultural practices, mores and issues. This understanding could be enhanced with the regular revising of an office resource file.

- **Celebrate good practice**

Smith (2009) points out that social work, in general, appears to be reluctant to celebrate achievement and innovation. One potential consequence of this in terms of social work with Gypsies, Roma and Travellers is the absence of good practice examples that could be used to feed into national or local policy. In order to develop this area of practice, social work organisations should consider publishing details of their work with Gypsies, Roma and Travellers so that others may use this information to develop their own approaches and learn from the lessons being discussed.

matters, this amounts to culturally incompetent care. The experience of culturally incompetent care can add to a sense of alienation, marginalisation and oppression.

To overcome these challenges, professionals and carers from the majority community must recognise that they might not know all of the answers to questions about Gypsy, Roma and Traveller cultures. However, they need to be able to place themselves in the role of a "student", ready to show a genuine interest in the child and the need to talk to and listen to them in order to learn about their culture and identity, and to be proactive in trying to find out more. Showing a genuine interest in them, not just as a child, but as a Gypsy, Roma and Traveller child, can help to develop pride in the richness and diversity of their cultural background and identity, and ultimately help the child to feel more comfortable in the placement. Such an approach will also offer a sense of safety so that the child can develop a feeling of trust in the Gypsy, Roma and Traveller/majority community relationship. Being culturally competent is not a one-off event, but a state of mind that recognises the importance of difference and demonstrates a commitment to learning, reflecting and sharing on an ongoing basis. It is about being sensitive to feelings of cultural displacement and trying to understand what this might feel like.

In the same way that social workers need to acknowledge the history of state oppression of Gypsy, Roma and Traveller communities, it is important that those providing direct care also understand this. Professionals and carers from the majority community are unlikely to be able to provide culturally competent care unless they are able to work within a human rights framework that recognises the historical, social and political oppression of Gypsy, Roma and Traveller communities. To ignore these matters is likely to be perceived as colluding with the ideas and ideology that underpin such oppression, and contribute to feelings of alienation, which in turn will have a negative impact on the development of a positive Gypsy, Roma and Traveller identity for the child.

MULTICULTURAL PLANNING

The second aspect of Vonk's (2001) culturally competent approach is a requirement for multicultural planning, which refers to 'the creation of avenues for the...child to learn about and participate in his or her culture of birth' and ideally involves 'direct involvement in the milieu of the birth culture'. In some ways, this can be seen as the practical application of the understanding and awareness already noted, and hopefully allows for further development and refinement of that understanding, including

Ideas for Gypsy, Roma and Traveller multicultural planning

Allen (2013) lists several techniques which can be employed to promote a positive Gypsy, Roma and Traveller identity.

- Participating in Gypsy, Roma and Traveller community events such as horse fairs and sales.

- Attending storytelling events, films and plays that are written and performed by Gypsy, Roma and Traveller community members.

- Providing a talking evening to enable the child to talk about their own family, culture, lived experiences, hopes, dreams and aspirations.

- Promoting positive Gypsy, Roma and Traveller role models such as sportspeople, artists, actors and community leaders.

- Having pictures, articles and artwork that reflect a positive view of Gypsy, Roma and Traveller communities and discussing these with the child.

- Accessing Gypsy, Roma and Traveller learning materials, including storybooks, articles and websites.

- Listening to Gypsy, Roma and Traveller music and encouraging the child to play the music, if they are interested in this.

- Watching documentaries about Gypsy, Roma and Traveller cultures and talking to the child about the accuracy of them.

- Commemorating International Holocaust Memorial Day and reminding the child about how this fits with Gypsy, Roma and Traveller history.

- Liaising with community representatives to organise visits with community members/campsites to learn about Gypsy, Roma and Traveller cultures.

- Inviting Gypsy, Roma and Traveller community representatives to the foster home/ residential home/school to talk about their own experiences and Gypsy, Roma and Traveller culture.

- Facilitating Gypsy, Roma and Traveller art and craft projects at home such as making paper flowers, flags and jewellery.

opportunities for Gypsy, Roma and Traveller children to find positive role models from within their own communities.

In part, multicultural planning for Gypsy, Roma and Traveller children will be about aiming to maximise continuity for the children entering care. This means that, wherever possible, schools and friendships should be maintained, as should contact with family members and the child's wider community. Not only is this essential in terms of reducing emotional distress, but it also reflects the need to ensure that children understand that, although they cannot live with their birth family, this does not imply a criticism of the wider Gypsy, Roma and Traveller community of which they are a part.

As with all children, it is also important to ensure that the child can minimise their own sense of disruption by being encouraged to take as many of their personal belongings as they want with them; this might include family photos, CDs, DVDs, posters, clothes, toys, bedding, trophies, and even pets. For Gypsy, Roma and Traveller children, the items that they take will likely reflect their Gypsy, Roma and Traveller heritage, and offer an opportunity for social workers and carers to communicate by their approach that they are interested in helping to maintain and learn about the child's Gypsy, Roma and Traveller culture.

It is important that multicultural planning is embedded in culturally competent care and not carried out in a way which could be construed as tokenistic. The activities themselves will be of most value where they take place in an environment where adults help the child make their own meanings about their heritage, and are sensitive about not "imposing" a culture onto a child. A culturally competent carer will be able to reflect with the child about the main differences between a Gypsy, Roma and Traveller and majority community culture, and about what this means to the child in their placement. Carers should never underestimate the power of talking to the child about their culture, identity and lived experiences.

CONTACT

Membership of a Gypsy, Roma and Traveller group is a unique and defining aspect of Gypsy, Roma and Traveller identity that for some is an essential element of belonging, positive self-esteem and emotional wellbeing. This means that promoting and facilitating contact is a crucial element within multicultural planning, but the issues are not always straightforward. Where any child has been removed from their birth parents because of harm that was done to them, any contact plan needs to be very carefully considered, but there are additional factors to consider with Gypsy, Roma and Traveller children and families.

- Gypsy, Roma and Traveller families are likely to be reluctant to engage with social workers, who they may perceive as agents of an oppressive state.

- Failure to achieve appropriate levels of contact will likely be distressing for children anyway, but might well be compounded if set against the background of cultural displacement.

Given these factors, social workers might need to make a particular effort to work in partnership with birth families, being respectful and sensitive to their past experiences and trying to gain a shared understanding about the benefits of contact in the context of cultural difference. To achieve this, social workers and others need to be empathic and active communicators who genuinely value the opportunities that the birth parents, extended family and community can offer in terms of helping the child to feel good about their Gypsy, Roma and Traveller heritage, amongst other benefits. This must also extend to social workers understanding that effective communication must also be sensitive to the communication preferences of those people whom they are working to support.

It is likely that social work practitioners will need to spend time with Gypsy, Roma and Traveller families to help them make sense of their own responses to interfamilial separation, enabling them to understand that their importance to their child does not diminish just because the child is in care. By empowering families to understand how contact can meet the developmental needs of the child, and by presenting this information in a way that is sensitive to a perception of majority community interference, feelings of reluctance on behalf of the parents can hopefully be minimised, and their sense of parental responsibility maximised. Where appropriate, it needs to be made clear that the family's capacity to recognise the needs of their child during contact will be an important component in any strategy for a return home.

As a cautionary note, it must be recognised that contact can at times be damaging and can re-traumatise a child. In line with best social work practice, specific attention must always be given to obtaining the child's views and opinions on the experience of contact, and the child's welfare and safety during contact must never be compromised. Where contact with parents is not in the best interest of children, exploring the possibility of contact with other family or community members is even more vital.

SURVIVAL SKILLS

In Vonk's (2001) framework, teaching survival skills refers to the need to prepare children to cope successfully with racism, including racial incidents, racially-based prejudice and discrimination:

> *Although it is not possible to protect children from racism, it is possible to help them actively cope with it. General strategies mentioned in the literature include learning how to talk about race and racism openly and honestly within the family, staying in touch with other families who are faced with similar issues, practising responses to insensitive comments from others, and demonstrating a lack of tolerance for any racially or ethnically biased comments.*

Vonk points out that although specific strategies will vary according to circumstance, it is important that children learn to verbalise rather than to internalise racism, have their feelings of anger and hurt validated, and hear the message that racism is unfair, but that they are not to blame for it. All of this is very relevant to Gypsy, Roma and Traveller children living in care, where they are likely to be victims of prejudice and bullying from the majority community (Allen, 2013). For Gypsy, Roma and Traveller children living in care with carers from the majority community, an associated survival skill will be about living as a member of two distinct communities with a history of mutual fear and suspicion. To achieve a positive identity, the child will need to make some sense of this without "taking sides" in a way that adversely impacts on their own sense of security and belonging.

Failure to achieve this will have an adverse impact on the Gypsy, Roma and Traveller child throughout their childhood. If they cannot feel comfortable within a majority community environment, they will be unlikely to settle in foster care or other settings, and their experience may be characterised by behavioural difficulties, poor educational achievement, feelings of isolation, and poor mental health. The impact may also be particularly evident when they transition out of care, and the risk for the child is that they grow up to feel that they are not a part of any community, and lack a strong cultural connection to either Gypsy, Roma and Traveller or majority community groups. This means that Gypsy, Roma and Traveller care leavers can often experience an insecure identity which locates them outside of both the dominant society and the Gypsy, Roma and Traveller community, leaving them feeling alienated and unwanted. Culturally competent practice ensures that children develop the skills required to function across both groups and to manage or cope with the challenges this brings.

TRAINING FOR CULTURAL COMPETENCE

While the most obvious way to address some of these challenges is to place Gypsy, Roma and Traveller children with appropriate carers in their own communities (see Chapter 9), the reality is that this is unlikely to happen for most children in the foreseeable future, and placement with families from the majority community by social workers from the same community is therefore inevitable. For this reason, it is essential that social workers, foster carers and others involved with Gypsy, Roma and Traveller children are trained in matters of anti-discriminatory practice and cultural competence.

Training programmes that take a reflective approach to cultural awareness-raising and engage with controversial areas such as oppression, sexism, racism, prejudice, cultural displacement, social marginalisation and forced eviction are recommended for those working with Gypsy, Roma and Traveller groups. Training must support practitioners to recognise that the structural challenges faced by individuals, families, groups and communities are not attributable to lifestyle choices, but rather to their disenfranchised position as distinct ethnic and cultural groups. Social work education must not collude with the perpetuation of inequality and disadvantage, and must seek to establish more challenging approaches that actively support anti-discriminatory and culturally competent practice.

As Coxhead (2007) and Hester (2004) have shown, these approaches are more likely to succeed if they are developed with strong support from trainers who are themselves skilled and expertly trained, and where significance is placed upon community participation. At their most effective, training programmes will be commissioned and delivered within broader organisational objectives, reinforced through well-supervised professional practice, and entail the involvement of community members in capacity-building projects. It is also important to remember that developing cultural competence does not depend on a one-off event or series of events, but is an ongoing process. It relies not only on an understanding of theoretical and structural aspects, but also on developing an understanding about day-to-day activities and rituals within a community.

An Munia Tober

Based in Belfast, An Munia Tober offers "Traveller Cultural and Racism Awareness Training" events that look at the culture, lifestyle and aspirations of Irish Travellers (visit www.anmuniatober.org for more information). The training covers issues such as:

- history, language and perceptions;
- the rich culture of Irish Travellers;
- differences and similarities with Romany Roma Gypsies;
- discrimination and racism;
- education, health and accommodation.

The College of Social Work also has an important role to play in the context of setting curriculum guidelines for social work educators. The College should ensure that providers of social work education include the position, experiences and perspectives of Gypsy, Roma and Traveller people within the consideration of other minoritised groups, as without this, social workers may remain indifferent to the challenges that Gypsies, Roma and Travellers face.

9

Placement issues

FAMILY AND FRIENDS CARE

In all four UK countries, there is a requirement that where a child is unable to live with a birth parent, then in the first instance consideration must be given to them living with a family member or friend. Although the legal frameworks are different in each country, they all allow for children to be placed directly from home, and require local authorities to provide appropriate support according to the circumstances of the case.

Family and Friends Care: Statutory guidance for local authorities (Department for Education, 2011)

This guidance – pertaining to England only – sets out a framework for the provision of support to family and friends carers. The guidance makes it clear that for children who are unable to live with their parents, they and their carers should receive the support they need to safeguard and promote their welfare, and this should not be determined by the legal status under which that care is offered. It requires local authorities to publish a family and friends policy setting out how they will meet their responsibilities, and briefly sets out the research evidence that family and friends care offers at least as good or better outcomes as other placement options.

Despite a significant amount of work that has been accomplished generally in relation to family and friends care/kinship care and the placement of children with people who are connected to the family (see Department for Education, 2011) it is unclear – due to a lack of research evidence – whether the same approach has been applied to Gypsy, Roma and Traveller children.

What we do know is that in spite of significant reservations about family and friends care from professionals historically, this has proved to be an effective placement option for numerous children, offering outcomes at least as good, often better, than any alternatives (Department for Education, 2011). The original opposition from social workers, often based on prejudice and stereotyping of the child's family of origin, has significantly reduced in the face of experience. It is nevertheless still widely believed that there is more scope for the effective use of family and friends care, and it is likely that Gypsy, Roma and Traveller children could potentially be beneficiaries in this regard. Family group conferences (as discussed in Chapter 7) can be used to good effect to identify suitable family and friends carers.

The obvious benefits of a good family and friends placement for a Gypsy, Roma or Traveller child will lie in the possibility of maintaining ongoing relationships, in addition to helping them to maintain a positive and developing Gypsy, Roma or Traveller identity. Where children are placed with carers from the majority community, promoting a positive cultural identity is always going to be challenging, and will demand considerable effort; for Gypsy, Roma or Traveller carers, this will happen naturally.

Family and friends care can provide a continuity that helps Gypsy, Roma or Traveller children to make sense of their family history, reduce the sense of separation and loss, provide the chance for permanence, and offer the opportunity for each person to build on these experiences to plan for their future. In the pursuit of culturally competent care, this opportunity should not be undervalued, particularly as it differs so starkly from the experience of emotional distress so often reported by those children who are living with foster carers from the majority community (Allen, 2013; O'Higgins, 1993).

ASSESSMENT AND SUPPORT

Despite the potential benefits of family and friends care for this group of children, assessing Gypsy, Roma or Traveller family and friends carers will bring with it challenges, and social workers may lack confidence or knowledge in working with this group. Many of the same issues that were discussed in relation to engaging with Gypsy, Roma or Traveller families (see Chapter 7) will equally apply in working with potential family and friends carers, and social workers will need to invest time in forming trusting relationships with those they are assessing. In addition, there may be ongoing legal processes to negotiate and, depending on the legal framework, it may be that family and friends carers need to be prepared to take on the role of foster carer, with all that this implies in relation to working with, and as part of, a state bureaucracy.

It is likely that assessing social workers will need to play an educative role, particularly if the family being assessed is unfamiliar with local government bureaucracy and regulation, as is likely to be the case. For Gypsy, Roma and Traveller family and friends carers, social workers may need to approach the meeting of legislative and local policy requirements in a flexible and proportionate way, keeping as a priority the needs of the individual child. This does not of course mean that the assessment should be any less rigorous than it would be for any other carer, and the same complexities that apply in relation to other family and friends care situations – keeping the child safe, appropriate discipline, managing contact, and working with the child's social worker – will all need careful consideration. There is anecdotal evidence that suggests that although this is not always easy, it can be achieved to good effect (see examples below).

Case example: accommodation

I worked with one family – they preferred the term Gypsy – who adopted two children from within their community.

The family were living in two caravans, which is the way for some communities – the adoptive mother and female children in one, adoptive father and boys in the other. This was causing difficulties for the adopted children, who struggled with the moves at bedtime, and at being separated from each other. I managed to get the local authority to give the funds to purchase a large mobile home on their site, arguing that if it was another family we would help to re-home them. There were then difficulties in sorting out the finances as they did not have a bank account and said they usually did business with a "spit and handshake", but the local authority accountants could not agree to this. There were also issues with financial assessments as all their work was cash in hand, and they needed the horses to be considered as a necessary expense due to their culture.

We did get it sorted, however, and the family moved in five months later. Working with Gypsies can be challenging as you have to research their lives and "walk in their shoes", but it can have successful outcomes. The children attended school, their attendance was excellent, and they were obviously very happy. I heard that things continued to go well for them, and every year I got a Christmas card until I left that local authority.

(Personal communication with Paul Adams)

Social workers will also need to think carefully about how they support family and friends carers, and will be required to act as a link between the family and the state bureaucracy that they represent. The nature of the support will need to be tailored to the specifics of the case, including the relevant legal framework.

Case example: being supportive

A number of my Gypsy, Roma and Traveller kinship carers do not read or write, and a number do not speak English, so good practice involves working flexibly and creatively. Limited literacy does not need to be a barrier or viewed as a deficiency in their good care of children. One of my English Gypsy carers uses a dictaphone for recording names, numbers and events, and several of my carers prefer to have contact with me by mobile, rather than by phoning the office.

When a new worker is allocated, I generally try to convene a meeting with the social worker and all the appropriate Gypsy Traveller Community, Health and Education workers, to start the process of beginning to learn about each other, and ways of working in a respectful and meaningful way. The balance between offering much-needed support and being patronising is very fine though. I regularly check out with my carers what support and advocacy they require, either with them or on their behalf.

(Personal communication with Paul Adams)

Support group for Travellers

In Cambridgeshire, a support group has been established with a group of five Traveller kinship carers. The organiser reports that the group has taken some time to become established because of practical difficulties in sharing information, linked with issues of literacy in a social care culture that relies on the written word. The group now meets on a monthly basis and has begun to form links with other kinship care support groups. The primary focus to date has been the opportunity for carers to share their difficult experiences of working with social services, and in making sense of a social care system that they have struggled to understand. This has included the opportunity to reflect on the cultural differences between the Travellers and social workers in relation to parenting expectations.

(Personal communication with Paul Adams)

FOSTERING

Gypsy, Roma and Traveller foster carers

As far as is known, there are very few Gypsy, Roma or Traveller foster carers in the UK who have been specifically approved to foster children from this community, except where they are known to the specific child as a family and friends foster carer. There are no specific projects along the lines of the Shared Rearing Project in the Republic of Ireland (see box later in this chapter), that was set up specifically to recruit and assess foster carers from the Travelling community. Consequently, when a Gypsy, Roma or Traveller child enters into care, they are unlikely to be fostered within their community, and their identity needs, views and wishes may not be fully accounted for if they are placed with foster carers from the majority community.

If there were Gypsy, Roma or Traveller foster carers available to foster children from these groups who were unable to live at home, this would allow those children to be looked after in settings where their cultural identity could most easily be promoted, in both the short and longer term. This was certainly the case for sibling group Lisa, Emma and Sarah in an Irish context (Allen, 2013).

> Emma: *When we moved to the Traveller foster family, it was very normal for us; we were just, like, "Oh yeah", and we became like daughters. We shared a room so we could spend time together. They understood us and treated us normal, like. Not like with settled carers. They didn't know us and tried to change us. With Traveller carers, you don't have to pretend you're something you're not.*

By living with a Traveller foster family, Lisa, Emma and Sarah were taught to maintain certain Travelling mores which were deemed essential for them to get married within the Travelling community, and they also talked about still feeling part of the Travelling community, for example, by visiting extended members of the foster family.

Within the UK, there is clearly scope for Gypsy, Roma and Traveller fostering to be developed, most likely by a specialist independent fostering provider, or by a consortium of local authorities, but at this time there is no indication that such work is taking place.

If a fostering service provider was interested in developing Gypsy, Roma and Traveller foster services, there would be a number of challenges that would need to be considered and addressed in relation to policy and practice, and individual assessment and support. These would probably include the following areas:

- attitudes to working with state organisations that are viewed as discriminating against and oppressing Gypsy, Roma and Traveller communities;

- willingness to be "monitored" by social workers from the majority community in relation to the standard of care being provided;

- willingness to adhere to state-imposed contact arrangements that might include prohibiting contact with birth parents;

- concepts of "nomadism", "accommodation", "address" and "household" and how these might be managed in a fostering context;

- attitudes to discipline and behaviour management in the context of legislation and local authority policies;

The Shared Rearing Project: Traveller fostering in the Republic of Ireland

In 1990, work was started to identify potential Traveller foster families who might be part of this project in Dublin where Traveller children would be fostered by carers who were not known to them, but who were from their own cultural community. By mid-1996, there were 11 approved Traveller families and they had fostered 34 children. Most of the foster families were living in standard housing, but had strong links with Travellers living in trailers, and many had grown up "on the road". The project was supported by a "cultural adviser" from the Traveller community.

Not surprisingly, there were challenges. There was the issue of matching to consider since where disagreements existed, these could be between extended families and run on for years, and it was important that children in care were not placed with people in conflict with their birth family.

There was also the fact that, for many Travellers, working with statutory services was completely new, and brought with it challenges for both parties. Traveller attitudes to education also needed to be considered, as for many families educating children over 12 at school was simply not seen as necessary. To require foster children to attend school would isolate them from other children in that family and wider community, but at the same time the law required school attendance. No foster carers were turned down simply because of their attitudes to education, but the issue was never entirely resolved.

There were, however, huge benefits. Some of the children's behaviour that had been considered difficult by foster carers from the majority community, such as shouting to be heard and engaging people with questions about their circumstances and relatives, were seen to be unproblematic and "normal" in a Traveller context. Similarly, contact meetings involving large groups of relatives were not viewed as cause for concern. It was reported that children settled quickly and remained or became located within their own community structures, and often previously unknown extended family members were identified during the placement.

A surprising benefit also emerged in that if placements became challenging, there was scope for children to move directly between the foster families in the project. Within the Traveller culture this was not viewed as problematic or as a failure, but was the norm for helping relatives through difficulties, with no sense that the main carers had in any way ceased to hold "parental authority". The most significant benefits for children were, however, in relation to helping them to handle discrimination and racism, and in supporting and developing pride in their identity as Travellers.

(Pemberton, 1999)

- attitudes to education of children, including school attendance and matters regarding sexual health and well-being;

- ability to participate in professional meetings and keep appropriate records;

- commitment to and ability to participate in foster carer training and development;

- arrangements for the payment of fostering allowances.

For some Gypsy, Roma and Traveller families, depending on their circumstances, none of these issues would be particularly problematic. However, as with the majority population, not everyone in the community will be suitable to be foster carers. In some situations there will be challenges that arise because fostering legislation, guidance and national minimum standards were not produced with Gypsy, Roma and Traveller carers in mind, and this may require fostering services to provide levels and types of support that may not be necessary for foster carers from the majority community, for example, around education, keeping records or sex education. It is important to recognise that any potential obstacles can be overcome in the same way they have been in the Republic of Ireland, where the Shared Rearing Project was developed in a state-structured framework, and there are also isolated examples of Gypsy foster carers having been approved in the UK (see box). It is generally accepted that foster carers need to be flexible, willing to reflect and adjust where they can, rather than holding rigid views and expectations. There is no reason to think that the same would not apply with Gypsy, Roma or Traveller carers.

A Gypsy foster carer's story

I travelled around a lot as a child. It didn't seem strange or unusual to me at all. I was a Gypsy, all of my friends and family were Gypsies and everyone moved around a lot. We would mainly travel in the warmer months and then settle for a while during the winter when my sisters and I would attend the local school. I remember this time as really happy, with lots of time to play and different places to explore.

We did occasionally come up against discrimination; sometimes people would shout things at us in the street or the other kids at school would call us names like "dirty Gypo". This never really bothered me though, as I was proud of who I was and knew what they were saying wasn't true.

When I was a teenager I started going to church and got to know lots of non-Gypsy people (Gorgios) and I became quite close to one particular family who had five young children. A year or so later, the parents were driving with the three younger children in the car and had a terrible accident in which they both died. I stayed in hospital with the three little ones and had to tell them that their parents were dead. A little while later, these children were all split up and sent to different foster placements. It was at this time I became really interested in being a foster carer but I didn't think that would be possible because I was too young and because I was a Gypsy.

In the years that followed, lots of things changed for me. Because of my involvement with a local church I got a job as a youth worker, which I really enjoyed. I also bought a house with my non-Gypsy partner, and this is when I started thinking about being a foster carer again. We approached an independent fostering service, and were assigned our own social worker who took the time to get to know us and answer all of the questions we had about being foster carers.

During this time, our social worker wanted to know all about our backgrounds, and I was a little bit nervous at first as I was so used to people discriminating against Gypsies and Travellers. I decided that I just needed to be open and honest with our social worker, who in turn was interested in, and respectful of, my background. I was never given the impression that being a Gypsy-Traveller would stand in the way of my becoming a foster carer. After several months' assessment and training, we were approved to foster up to three children.

I've been fostering for several years now and it is the hardest but also the most rewarding thing I've ever done. The children I've looked after have been very difficult at times but this is to be expected when you consider the things that have happened that have brought them into care.

My family has been brilliant with the children I've fostered. This is a new experience for them too as, like me, they had never heard of a Gypsy being a foster carer. The children have all been welcomed with open arms and included fully into the family. At Christmas, they all get the same presents as my nieces and nephews who think of the children I foster as their new cousins. My extended family and community have also been really positive and proud of me for making a difference in the lives of vulnerable children.

So far, I have never fostered a child who has come from the Gypsy-Traveller community but I like to think that if I did, I would have a real understanding of their background. If more Gypsies and Travellers were aware that fostering and adoption was an option for them and they knew they would not be discriminated against or looked down on by social services, this would be a step in the right direction. The Gypsy community really values and cares for their children and shouldn't be discounted when those same children require foster care or adoption.

(Personal communication with Paul Adams)

Michael's story

For Irish Traveller Michael, the opportunity to live with Traveller carers empowered him to feel psychologically connected to them – a feeling that he explains was missing when he was living with settled carers.

Michael: *When I went to the foster carers in the Travelling community, I could relate to them that bit better as opposed to settled people. I stayed with a settled couple there for a year prior to coming to my Traveller foster carers and I found it OK, like, it was good but I suppose you just connect that much better to the Travelling community as opposed to settled people, you know? Yeah, I do think so, yeah, yeah, because I could relate to them more so, as opposed to settled people, they knew my kind of surroundings before I went into care, not the bad side of things of course, but in general, it is a different way of going on. Some settled people wouldn't understand our way of going on as opposed to Traveller people. You relate to them on a positive note, so yeah, I found it helpful.*

Interviewer: *Do you think that your relationship with your family has been made easier because you were adopted by a Travelling family?*

Michael: *Yeah, yeah, definitely. To be fair to my biological family, they do kind of respect my foster carers for taking me in. Absolutely. As I have said, there have been plenty of cases where Traveller kids are not allowed to see their biological family. Even the time we got adopted, we kept my surname. We didn't change because my carers knew that that is my name and I suppose my biological family saw that and respected that. For us Travellers, changing your name is a lot to ask because that is something that makes you a Traveller. Who you are. Everyone is happy on all accounts. I think that my foster parents being Travellers definitely helped.*

(Allen, 2013)

Foster carers from the majority community

The current reality is that there are very few Gypsy, Roma or Traveller foster carers, and the vast majority of children from Gypsy, Roma or Traveller backgrounds who cannot live with birth parents or extended family will be placed with foster carers from the majority community. Where this is the case, those carers need to be assessed, supervised and supported in a way that promotes culturally competent practice (see Chapter 8) and with social workers operating within an anti-discriminatory framework (see Chapter 7). For both foster carers and social workers, that will almost certainly mean the need for specific training around working with Gypsy, Roma and Traveller families, a children's rights approach, and the development of links with an appropriate Gypsy, Roma or Traveller community. It is likely that fostering Gypsy, Roma and Traveller children will be experienced by foster carers as being different from fostering other children (see box below), and will bring with it certain challenges.

Fostering Gypsy children: a personal story

We are not from a Gypsy background, but we have fostered a lot of Gypsy children over the years, all of them boys aged between about three and ten years old. Each time the boys have moved on, they have left a huge gap in our lives; they were all lovely, vulnerable lads, and we keep in touch with a number of them. They did bring plenty of challenges though!

The most problematic characteristic was running off and being away from us. This didn't seem like a hostile act, just something they felt more comfortable with, and the many acres of our large rural property was never enough. It was as if the boys just couldn't keep still, and I regularly received telephone calls from neighbours and others saying they had found one of the boys somewhere in the community. We soon learned that "chasing" the children was counterproductive, but as foster carers it was sometimes difficult managing requirements about missing children when this was the norm for most days. In an attempt to keep one of the boys closer to home, we built a treehouse in the garden. This worked to a degree, but I still struggled to get him to come in to eat and often resorted to giving him his meals in the treehouse!

We found that the boys were all very good horsemen, and seemed very natural with our horse and pony. Risk assessments were based on riding correctly and under supervision but the boys did not follow these rules! They just didn't seem afraid of falling off, and we also noticed that for younger ones learning to ride a bike seemed to come easily and with little adult input. In fact, the boys were all very agile, running, jumping and climbing, and could have been excellent sportsmen had they been more disciplined and willing to comply with the rules of team games. Two of the boys were particularly talented footballers but our efforts to promote this proved unsuccessful as they struggled with the organised nature of the activity.

Although the boys all had some charming and loveable aspects, it felt as if they had been raised to be strong and at times aggressive. We had to work hard to prevent physical bullying of other children and overly aggressive training of our dogs, as well as trying to make play-fighting safe and manageable. We also tried to address unkind comments about and to girls and disabled people that made us feel uncomfortable.

The boys seemed to think that they were older than they really were, at times behaving like teenagers but at other times reverting to be much younger children, such as at bathtime and bedtime. They seemed to have a sense of being responsible, and as they got a bit older needing to be strong and capable to protect their families, even though they were only children. We have older boys, and this was really helpful as the foster children looked up to them and seemed keen to spend time with them.

It really helped living rurally, as the noise levels were often high! We needed to have a thick skin as we were criticised a lot, and we had to learn to accept and promote community links. All of the boys had a real pride in their heritage, and thought that the Gypsy way was the right way. As foster carers, we learned to accept that, and to accept the children for who they were. We often talk about incidents that happened with these boys, sometimes with horror but more often with pleasure, and one thing is for sure, they will never be forgotten by us, our family, friends and neighbours.

(Personal communication with Paul Adams)

Preparing Gypsy, Roma and Traveller children to move into a house

Allen (2013) explains that where Gypsy, Roma or Traveller children are being placed into care, it is important not to assume that they will know about living in a house, or will have ever been in a house before. Carers living in houses should address these matters by talking to the child about how the foster home might be different to the home that they lived in before coming into care. Photographs could be used to prepare and enable children to see their new home, their bedroom, the stairs, kitchen and bathroom in advance of moving in. Discussions could helpfully take place with birth parents about washing arrangements that the children are familiar with in an effort to maintain existing practices as much as is possible in the new home, and to avoid teaching children habits that might be frowned upon if they return to their parents or community. Foster carers also need to be sensitive to the fact that the "house" might be experienced as oppressing or containing, and for older children in particular, could represent a symbol of anti-Gypsy, Roma and Traveller control.

ADOPTION AND PERMANENCE

Adoption and other legal frameworks for permanence are generally accepted as offering children the best long-term outcomes in that they can offer stability, security and good attachment, while minimising the likelihood of disruption. They also often allow for decisions about the child to be taken by a person or people who love them and want what is best for them, rather than a state official acting as a corporate parent. A good permanent placement allows the child to become a fully integrated and valued family member with the associated emotional security that comes with this.

Adoption and other permanent arrangements are meant to offer a family for life, and for the adult or adults to become primary attachment figures for the child. In terms of identity, it is anticipated that the child will – according to their age and experience – begin to take on aspects of their new family identity, in the same way that everyone's identity changes to reflect a range of different experiences and relationships over time. In birth families, it is normal for the child to grow up with a single family identity, where genetic inheritance and subsequent experience are often connected. For adopted children, they will always be part of two families (even if they have little or no contact with one of them), and their identity will grow to reflect aspects of both families, to greater or lesser degrees.

For Gypsy, Roma and Traveller children, an adoptive or permanent placement with a Gypsy, Roma or Traveller family will allow for an identity that emerges in a context where their Gypsy, Roma or Traveller heritage is reflected by their lived experience, as well as their genetic make-up. Being Gypsy, Roma or Traveller will be felt positively and promoted in the context of day-to-day life. This is an argument in favour of efforts to recruit Gypsy, Roma and Traveller adopters as well as foster carers, and the potential difference this can make is highlighted in the contrasting testimonies of Michael and Josephine, as set out in this chapter.

For a Gypsy, Roma and Traveller child placed with parents or carers from the majority community, the issues are less straightforward. It is expected that the primary aim for adopted children is to become attached to and a full part of their new family, legally and emotionally "owned" by that new family. At the same time, it is recognised that these children have a birth family, and they need to make sense of their past, while at the same time moving on from it. For children placed with adopters from the same ethnic and cultural background, the issues about their heritage are usually very specific to their original family, and the questions they have will be about their birth family as individuals, why they could not live with them, where they are now, etc. For Gypsy, Roma and Traveller children (and some other transracially placed groups), it is likely that there will be additional questions about what it means to be Gypsy, Roma or Traveller, and possibly thoughts about what they might have lost in terms of their culture of birth. While a culturally competent approach will be necessary to try and address those issues, we should not underestimate how challenging that might be in the context of permanence, which expects the child to be more closely connected to the values and culture of their new family than is the case with non-permanent care arrangements.

An adopter's story

On the day that I was approved to adopt, I was given information about my son Peter. He was nearly six years old and his birth parents and ancestors were Gypsies. I was told that Peter's birth family was viewed negatively within the Gypsy community due to their lifestyle and choices, and that Peter – who is developmentally delayed – did not understand his heritage, and he did not know his parents were Gypsies.

Peter's heritage did not concern me, and by that I mean I did not feel negatively about the Travelling/Gypsy community. I was conscious of the importance of promoting his identity and heritage, although I was advised by Peter's social worker that his birth parents did not promote a Gypsy identity. I did carry out some internet research to try and find some information about culture and lifestyle; however, this wasn't very successful. I found some websites for children in the hope they could be helpful for Peter. I remember being asked about his heritage at the approval panel and saying that I had carried out some research and planned on working out the most effective way of supporting Peter to feel positive about his heritage. I meant what I said, but a number of things have made that difficult.

When Peter came home to me, it became evident that he was very developmentally delayed, and I had to focus on supporting him to settle and to manage day-to-day life and activities. I have worked very hard at promoting attachment and resilience, and he had to move schools which caused massive stress for him. It has not felt like he was able to deal with thinking about less immediate matters like culture and heritage.

Also, although Peter knew little about the life experiences of his birth family, he did have very bad memories and was scared they would find him and hurt him. This made it difficult to raise the subject of his background with him. When I formally adopted Peter, I asked him if he wished to keep his birth family name as a middle name; he was adamant that he did not, and was angry with me for suggesting it. I would have agreed to letterbox contact with Peter's birth parents, but they did not wish to have any contact with social workers.

Shortly after placement I read a story in the local newspaper about a Gypsy family with the same family name as Peter, who were convicted of a violent crime, and I became concerned about maintaining his anonymity. Peter also disclosed some potentially identifying information to his school class and that made me more worried, particularly as his father had threatened to take him from foster care and disappear.

Where we live, the Travelling community is often discriminated against, and this has also been another factor in my approach. Peter has difficulties at school due to his behaviour, and other parents don't wish their children to play with him. I am concerned that being open about his heritage could lead to further discrimination. At his stage of development, I don't think he understands the significance of heritage and culture, but the stereotyping does make me feel sad for Peter.

I would have liked to have received some information and guidance on promoting Peter's heritage and culture, and would have made this a priority had he already had some understanding about it. I was given a comprehensive reading list about trauma, attachment and resilience, but nothing about the Travelling community. The dilemma for me has been how to promote culture and heritage whilst also keeping him safe. I do not know if he would be welcome in the Travelling community due to his family, whom I believe have been shunned. I am not saying that I think the Travelling community poses a bigger risk or danger than the non-Traveller community, but the risks in this particular family are very real.

That said, I do feel guilty that I haven't promoted Gypsy culture and heritage and I plan on completing a detailed life story book for Peter this year, where I will acknowledge his heritage fully. I think it is very important for Peter to know his heritage, and I don't plan on hiding this from him, but I am mindful of his safety and him understanding how to keep himself safe. I do educate him on general identity, culture and religious beliefs, and the importance of equality and diversity, so I'm hoping that when I discuss his heritage he will respond positively.

(Personal communication with Paul Adams)

LEAVING CARE

Research evidence about the situation of Gypsy, Roma and Traveller children leaving care is limited, with the notable exceptions of O'Higgins (1993), Pemberton (1999) and Allen (2013). Not surprisingly, the limited evidence does suggest that for those Gypsy, Roma and Traveller children who return from care to a Gypsy, Roma or Traveller culture and lifestyle, being isolated from that whilst living in care can have a longlasting and harmful impact on that individual's life.

Thinking about leaving care raises important questions about care planning more generally for Gypsy, Roma and Traveller children, and requires social workers to be thinking at an early stage about the likely life trajectory of a child coming into the care system. The way that the Gypsy, Roma or Traveller identity of a child is supported and promoted will be very different for a baby with a care plan of adoption, compared to an older teenager who has always lived in a Gypsy, Roma or Traveller community. Where it is clear that a child is going to live as an adult within a Gypsy, Roma or Traveller community, then preparation for that will need to start from the day they come into care, and not wait for an arbitrary date when pathway planning begins.

For the transition out of care and back to a Gypsy, Roma or Traveller community to be effective, where that is the plan, it is evident that cultural continuity throughout care represents an essential aspect in the development and formation of a secure identity as a Gypsy, Roma or Traveller adult. In such a scenario, it is essential that Gypsy, Roma and Traveller children experience continued cultural inclusion, and this cannot happen without significant interaction with Gypsy, Roma or Traveller communities. Most obviously, this will be best achieved by a placement with Gypsy, Roma or Traveller carers, but where that is not possible, there is a need for social workers and others to forge and maintain relationships with a Gypsy, Roma or Traveller community.

Josephine's story

Josephine was adopted as a baby from a Showman family, and brought up by parents from the majority community. At the age of 11, she discovered adoption papers stating that her birth family were Travellers. She left home at 16 and took to the road in search of her family and by the age of 23 had bought a trailer and was struggling to survive in a society peppered with anti-Gypsy, Roma and Traveller racism. Having been raised in care, she had not been taught the key skills needed to live in this world, and over time she experienced violent eviction, exploitation and the removal of her own children into care.

Despite these extreme challenges, Josephine was driven by a determination and commitment to find her birth family. However, her attempts to integrate with the Traveller community were rejected as she was perceived to be a masquerading imposter. Eventually she had to accept that she was unable to be part of the community that she longed to be with because of the simple fact that she had been brought up by non-Traveller parents. In her own words:

I have been unable to find my birth parents. This has left me needing to do this before they die and it will help me more emotionally and it is something that I need to do to grow into a more confident person. As a Showman being in care, I felt great separation and loss and having no knowledge of your roots rips you inside and causes a massive hole. I have no proper identity. I'm like a jigsaw with the pieces missing. My soul yearns to belong and to understand more, and to find the missing pieces will make me achieve more emotional stability. I've grown up but there are pieces missing, aren't there. One of my main dreams is to find my dad and mum. It is part of my world of hope and future. I need this to settle the hole in my soul. Just a cuddle from Dad and Mum would help me cope with my future and bring forgiveness and understanding. Maybe create emotional stability within myself.

(Allen, 2013)

10
Conclusions

THEMES

There are a number of themes that run throughout this good practice guide that are worth bringing together.

- Gypsy, Roma and Traveller is an umbrella term that covers a wide range of groups, families and individuals, each with their own distinct histories, cultures and beliefs.

- Methods for collecting data about the number of Gypsies, Roma and Travellers in the UK are fundamentally flawed, and so there is a lack of knowledge, including of the numbers of Gypsy, Roma and Traveller children in the care system.

- Gypsies, Roma and Travellers are an oppressed group who historically and currently face social and economic discrimination and oppression from state bureaucracies in a number of ways.

- Good practice therefore requires social care agencies to acknowledge oppression, and to take proactive steps to meaningfully engage with Gypsy, Roma and Traveller communities, both collectively and individually.

- Although the evidence is limited, there are strong indications that Gypsy, Roma and Traveller children have a particularly poor experience of the care system, in which issues of identity and culture are not well addressed.

- Romani Gypsy, Irish Travellers and Scottish Gypsy/Travellers are legally defined as an ethnic group and specific equality legislation is applicable. Child care legislation across the UK also requires practitioners to take account of culture and diversity when working with children and families.

- Good social work will only be possible in a context that promotes children's rights, and recognises the need for advocacy and empowerment.

- The concept of cultural competence is central to effectively meeting the needs of Gypsy, Roma and Traveller children and families.

- Where children need to come into care, the use of family and friends carers must be fully explored, both to comply with the law but also to meet the needs of the children concerned.

- There are a number of potential benefits from recruiting adopters and foster carers from Gypsy, Roma and Traveller communities.

RECOMMENDATIONS FOR POLICY MAKERS

- Gypsy, Roma and Traveller communities and their representatives should be much more involved in all aspects of policy making. This could be achieved by developing and utilising consultation networks.

- Further research should be commissioned to look into the social care needs of Gypsy, Roma and Traveller children and families, and the care experiences of this group of children.

- Consideration should be given to asking Ofsted/the Children's Right's Director to report on the care experiences of children from Gypsy, Roma and Traveller communities.

- In devising curricula for social work courses, the College of Social Work should consider the need for effective social work practice with Gypsy, Roma and Traveller communities.

- The recommendations set out below in respect of local authorities should be set out as requirements in appropriate legislation or statutory guidance.

RECOMMENDATIONS FOR LOCAL AUTHORITIES

- Local authorities should set up systems to gather accurate and detailed data in relation to Gypsy, Roma and Traveller children and families in their area, including those children living in care.

- Local authorities should develop a specific local policy setting out how they will meet the needs of Gypsy, Roma and Traveller children and families in their area, including issues of accommodation.

- Local authorities should have a named senior manager with responsibility for implementing and evaluating social work practice with Gypsy, Roma and Traveller children and families.

- The named senior manager should be required to make efforts to engage with local Gypsy, Roma and Traveller communities, and to consult them in relation to the recommended local policy.

- Local authorities should put in place arrangements for social workers and other staff to access specialist advice and resources when working with Gypsy, Roma and Traveller children and families.

- Appropriate and relevant training should be made available to all children's social workers, independent reviewing officers and others who are working to support Gypsy, Roma and Traveller children.

RECOMMENDATIONS FOR FOSTERING AND ADOPTION SERVICES

- Independent fostering providers and voluntary adoption agencies should consider the feasibility of setting up specialist services to recruit, assess and approve foster carers and adopters from the Gypsy, Roma and Traveller communities.

- Local authority fostering and adoption services should also consider specific efforts to recruit foster carers and adopters from Gypsy, Roma and Traveller communities, either through consortium working or individually (if they have sufficient demand or reason to justify this).

- Appropriate and relevant training should be made available to all social workers, foster carers, adopters and others who are working with or parenting Gypsy, Roma and Traveller children.

RECOMMENDATIONS FOR PRACTITIONERS

- Individual social workers, foster carers and adopters should take personal responsibility for practising or parenting in a culturally competent way.

- Individual social workers should take personal responsibility for ensuring that they practise within an anti-discriminatory framework, and in accordance with the requirements of their regulatory body around issues of culture, equality and diversity.

Given the disenfranchised position of Gypsy, Roma and Traveller communities, and the various demands on local authority resources, it is unlikely that the positive changes recommended in this practice guide will come easily or quickly. More immediately, it is hoped that there will be recognition that the challenges faced by Gypsy, Roma and Traveller children and families are not attributed to a lifestyle choice, but rather reflect their oppressed position in society underpinned by an ideology that works against Gypsy, Roma and Traveller people.

However, opportunities do exist for good social work practice, and there are already some examples of this with particular Gypsy, Roma and Traveller families or groups. By rising to the challenges set out in this good practice guide, local authorities and individual social workers can do more to empower Gypsy, Roma and Traveller children and families to lead lives where Gypsy, Roma and Traveller culture and identity is valued and promoted. It seems appropriate that the final word should go to a Traveller who has been in care. Michael (in Allen, 2013) gives the following advice:

> *To all Travellers and Gypsies in care, have an open mind and hope that your foster carers have a good understanding of who you are and where you come from. Be grateful that they are out for you. Hope that they are aware of where you are from and that you have seen violence, drink, drugs, and sadness. You will be a better person in the long run. You might think that they are strict. You may be used to running the streets all night, but their rules are for a good cause. It is only when you are older that you will realise that they are looking out for you. My love goes out to you.*

Useful organisations

Brent Irish Advisory Service (BIAS)
The Old Library Building
Willesden Green Library Centre
95 High Road
London NW10 2SF
Tel: 020 8459 66 55
www.biasbrent.co.uk

Bromley Gypsy/Traveller Project
230 Sandway Road
St Mary Cray
Orpington
Kent BR5 3TF
Tel: 01689 839052

Cambridgeshire Travellers' Advocacy Service
Working for Travellers' Rights
Cambridgeshire Travellers Initiative
Travellers Advocacy Service
7e High Street
Fenstanton
Cambridgeshire PE28 9LQ
Tel: 01480 496577
Email: advocacy@ormiston.org
www.ormiston.org/community/opus24.html

The Children's Society
Edward Rudolf House
Margery Street
London WC1X 0JL
Tel: 0845 300 1128
www.childrenssociety.org.uk

Derbyshire Gypsy Liaison Group (DGLG)
Unit 3, Molyneux Business Park
Whitworth Road
Darley Dale
Matlock
Derbyshire DE4 2HJ
Tel: 01629 732744
www.dglg.org

Doncaster CVS
'Give us a Voice' Gypsy and Traveller Forum
5–6 Trafford Court
Doncaster DN1 1PN
Tel: 01302 343300 (ext 280)
www.doncastercvs.org.uk

Friends, Families and Travellers
113 Queen's Road
Brighton
East Sussex BN1 3XG
Tel: 01273 234777
Email: fft@gypsy-traveller.org
www.gypsy-traveller.org/

Gypsy Council
Tel: 07963 565952
Email: info@gypsy-association.com
www.gypsy-association.co.uk

Gypsy Roma Traveller History Month
http://grthm.natt.org.uk

Leeds GATE (Gypsy and Traveller Exchange)
Tel: 0113 240 2444
Email: info@leedsgate.co.uk
www.leedsgate.co.uk

The Gypsy Council
Tel: 01708 868986
www.thegypsycouncil.org

Irish Community Care Merseyside: Working with Irish Travellers
Tel: 0151 237 3987
www.iccm.org.uk/

The Irish Traveller Movement in Britain
The Resource Centre
356 Holloway Road
London N7 6PA
Tel: 020 7607 2002
Email: info@irishtraveller.org.uk
www.irishtraveller.org.uk

Leicester Gypsy Council Liaison Group
Rosevale House
Hinkley Road
Sapcote LE9 4LH
Tel: 07838 340371 (ask for Alfie Kefford, chairman)

London Gypsy Traveller Unit
Tel: 020 8533 2002
www.lgtu.org.uk

The National Bargees Traveller Association
30 Silver Street
Reading
Berkshire RG1 2ST
Tel: 0118 321 4128
Email: secretariat@bargee-traveller.org.uk
www.bargee-traveller.org.uk

National Federation of Gypsy Liaison Groups
Unit 3, Molyneux Business Park
Whitworth Road
Darley Dale
Matlock
Derbyshire DE4 2HJ
Tel: 01629 760435
Email: info@nationalgypsytravellerfederation.org
www.nationalgypsytravellerfederation.org

National Romani Gypsy and Traveller Alliance
Roma Support Group
PO Box 23610
London E7 0XB
Email: info@romasupportgroup.org.uk
www.romasupportgroup.org.uk

Roma Support Group
PO Box 23610
London E7 0XB
Email: info@romasupportgroup.org.uk
www.romasupportgroup.org.uk

Sheffield Gypsy and Traveller Support Group
Tel: 0114 279 8236 (ask for Chrissy Meledy)
Email: sheffieldgypsy.travellersupport@virgin.net

Southwark Traveller Action Group (STAG)
The Willowbrook Centre
48 Willowbrook Road
London SE15 6BW
Tel: 020 7277 6172
www.travellersite.org

South West Alliance of Nomads (SWAN)
Tel: Paul Clark on 07948 123330
Email: secretary@gypsytravellerhelp.org
www.gypsytravellerhelp.org

Sussex Traveller Action Group (STAG)
Email: info@sussextag.org.uk
www.sussextag.org.uk
www.gypsytravellerhelp.org

Travellers Advice Team
(part of the Community Law Partnership)
4th Floor, Ruskin Chambers
191 Corporation Street
Birmingham B4 6RP
Advice line: 0121 685 8677
Tel: 0121 685 8595
Email: office@communitylawpartnership.co.uk
www.communitylawpartnership.co.uk

The Travellers Aid Trust

PO Box 16

Kidwelly

Carmarthenshire SA17 5BN

Tel/Fax: 01554 891876

Email: info@travellersaidtrust.org

http://travellersaidtrust.org/

The Traveller Law Reform Project

c/o London Gypsy and Traveller Unit

6 Westgate Street

London E8 3RN

Email: info@travellerslaw.org.uk

TravellerSpace

TI Champions Yard

Causewayhead

Penzance

Cornwall TR18 2TA

Tel: 01736 366940

Email: tspace@travellerspace-cornwall.org

Travellers' Times

The Rural Media Company

Sullivan House

72–80 Widemarsh Street

Hereford HR4 9HG

Tel: 01432 344039

Email: travellerstimes@ruralmedia.co.uk

www.travellerstimes.org.uk

York Travellers Trust

Tel: 01904 630526

http://yorktravellerstrust.wordpress.com/

Bibliography

Acton T (1974) *Gypsy Politics and Social Change*, London: Routledge and Kegan Paul

Acton T (1994) 'Modernisation, moral panics and the Gypsies', *Sociology Review*, 4:1, pp. 24–28

Acton T (ed) (2000) *Scholarship and the Gypsy Struggle: Commitment in Romani studies*, Hatfield: University of Hertfordshire Press

Acton T and Mundy G (eds) (1997) *Romani Culture and Gypsy Identity*, Hatfield: University of Hertfordshire Press

Allen D (2012) 'Gypsies, Travellers and social policy: misconceptions and insignificance', in Richardson J and Ryder A (eds) *Gypsies and Travellers: Accommodation, empowerment and inclusion in British society*, Bristol: Policy Press

Allen D (2013, unpublished) *Changing Relationships with the Self and Others: An interpretative phenomenological analysis of a Traveller and Gypsy life in public care*, Leicester: De Montfort University

Bailey R and Brake M (eds) (1980) *Radical Social Work and Practice*, London: Edward Arnold

Bhopal K (2011) '"This is a school, it's not a site": teachers' attitudes towards Gypsy and Traveller pupils in schools in England, UK', *British Educational Research Journal*, 37:3, pp. 465–483

Bowers J (2009) *Guide to Working with Gypsies and Travellers*, accessed 21 September 2012, at: www.ccinform.co.uk/articles/2009/10/21/3811/guide+to+working+with+gypsies+and+travellers.html

British Waterways (2011) *Guidance for Boaters without a Home Mooring*, accessed 11 February 2013, at www.waterscape.com/media/documents/1862.pdf

Brown P and Niner P (2009) *Assessing Local Housing Authorities' Progress in Meeting the Accommodation Needs of Gypsy and Traveller Communities in England*, Manchester: Equality and Human Rights Commission

Butler J (1983) *Gypsies and the Personal Social Services* (social work monograph), Norwich, University of East Anglia

Cemlyn S (1998) *Policy and Provision by Social Services for Traveller Children and Families: Report on research study*, Bristol: University of Bristol Press

Cemlyn S (2000a) 'Assimilation, control, mediation or advocacy? Social work dilemmas in providing anti-oppressive services for Traveller children and families', *Child and Family Social Work*, 5:4, pp. 327–41

Cemlyn S (2000b) 'From neglect to partnership? Challenges for social services in promoting the welfare of Traveller children', *Child Abuse Review*, 9:5, pp. 349–63

Cemlyn S (2006) 'Human rights and Gypsies and Travellers: an exploration of the application of a human rights perspective to social work with a minority community in Britain', *British Journal of Social Work*, advance release, pp. 1–21

Cemlyn S (2008) 'Human rights and Gypsies and Travellers: an exploration of the application of a human rights perspective to social work with a minority community in Britain', *British Journal of Social Work*, 38:1, pp. 153–173

Cemlyn S and Briskman L (2002) 'Social welfare within a hostile state', *Social Work Education*, 21:1, pp. 49–69

Cemlyn S, Greenfields M, Burnett S, Matthews Z and Whitwell C (2009) *Inequalities Experienced by Gypsy and Traveller Communities: A review*, Manchester: Equality and Human Rights Commission

Commission for Racial Equality (CRE) (2004) *Gypsies and Travellers: A strategy for the CRE 2004–2007*, London: CRE

Commission for Racial Equality (CRE) (2006) *Common Ground: Equality, good race relations and sites for Gypsies and Irish Travellers – report of a CRE inquiry in England and Wales*, London: CRE

Cook J, Dwyer P and Waite L (2010) 'The experiences of Accession 8 migrants in England: motivations, work and agency', *International Migration*, 49, pp. 54–79

Cowan D and Lomax D (2003) 'Policing unauthorised camping', *Journal of Law and Society*, 30:2, pp. 283–308

Coxhead J (2007) T*he Last Bastion of Racism?: Gypsies, Travellers and policing*, London: Institute of Education Press

Cummins S, Stafford M, Macinyre S, Marmot M and Ellaway A (2005) 'Neighbourhood environment and its association with self-rated health: evidence from Scotland and England', *Journal of Epidemiology and Community Health*, 59:3, pp. 207–13

Dawson R (2000) *Crime and Prejudice: Traditional Travellers*, Derby: Robert Dawson

Department for Children, Schools and Families (2007) *Elective Home Education: Guidelines for local authorities*, London: DCSF

Department for Communities and Local Government (2007) *Consultation on Revised Planning Guidance in Relation to Travelling Showpeople*, London: DCLG

Department for Communities and Local Government (2012) *Progress Report by the Ministerial Working Group on Tackling Inequalities Experienced by Gypsies and Travellers*, London: DCLG

Department for Education (2010) *The Children Act 1989 Guidance and Regulations. Volume 2: Care planning, placement and case review*, London: DfE

Department for Education (2011) *Family and Friends Care: Statutory guidance for local authorities*, London: DfE

Department for Education (2012) *Advice on School Attendance*, London: DfE

Department for Education and Skills (2003) *Aiming High: Raising the achievement of Gypsy Traveller pupils*, London: DfES

Derrington C (2007) 'Fight, flight and playing white: an examination of coping strategies adopted by Gypsy Traveller adolescents in English secondary schools', *International Journal of Educational Research*, 46:6, pp. 357–367

Derrington C and Kendall S (2004) *Gypsy Traveller Students in Secondary Schools: Culture, identity and achievement*, Stoke on Trent: Trentham Books

Derrington C and Kendall S (2007) 'Challenges and barriers to secondary education: the experiences of young Gypsy Traveller students in English secondary schools', *Social Policy and Society*, 7:1, pp. 119–28

Dingwall R, Eekelaar J and Murray T (1983) *The Protection of Children: State intervention and family life*, Oxford: Blackwell

Earle F, Dearling A, Whittle H, Glasse R and Gubby (1994) *A Time to Travel? An introduction to Britain's newer Travellers*, Lyme Regis: Enabler

Environment, Food and Rural Affairs Committee (2012) www.parliament.uk. Accessed 12 March 2013, from *Written Evidence Submitted by National Bargee Travellers Association*, www.publications.parliament.uk/pa/cm201213/cmselect/cmenvfru/1890/1890we07.htm

European Dialogue (2009) *Mapping Survey of A2 and A8 Roma in England*, London: prepared for the DCSF by European Dialogue

Exchange House Travellers Service (2004) *The Horsemen Project*, Dublin: Exchange House Travellers Service

Ferguson H (2011) *Child Protection Practice*, Hampshire: Palgrave Macmillan

Fisher I (2003) *Deprivation and Discrimination faced by Traveller Children: Implications for social policy and social work* (social work monograph), Norwich: University of East Anglia

Fraser A (1995) *The Gypsies*, Oxford: Blackwell Publishers

Garrett PM (2002) '"No Irish Need Apply": social work in Britain and the history and politics of exclusionary paradigms and practices', *British Journal of Social Work*, 32, pp. 477–94

Garrett PM (2004a) *Social Work and Irish People in Britain*, Bristol: Policy Press

Garrett PM (2004b) 'The electronic eye: emerging surveillant practices in social work with children and families', *European Journal of Social Work*, 7:1, pp. 57–71

Garrett PM (2005) 'Irish social workers in Britain and the politics of (mis) recognition', *British Journal of Social Work*, 16, pp. 1–18

Greenfields M (2002, unpublished PhD) *The Impact of Section 8 Children Act Applications on Travelling Families*, Bath: University of Bath

Greenfields M (2006) 'Gypsies, Travellers and legal matters', in Clark C and Greenfields M (eds) *Here to Stay: The Gypsies and Travellers of Britain*, Hatfield: University of Hertfordshire Press, pp. 133–81

Greenfields M and Smith D (2010) 'Housed Gypsy Travellers, social segregation and the reconstruction of communities', *Housing Studies*, 25:3, pp. 397–412

Guy W (1975) 'Ways of looking at Roms: the case of Czechoslovakia', in Rehfisch F (ed) *Gypsies, Tinkers and Other Travellers*, London: Academic Press

Gypsy Roma Traveller Leeds (2013) 'Gypsy Roma Traveller Leeds: communities around the world', in *Roma Traveller Leeds: The permanent site of the Gypsy Roma Traveller Communities*, accessed 9 March 2013, at www.grtleeds.co.uk/Culture/romaGypsies.html

Hancock I (2002) *We are the Romani People*, Hatfield: University of Hertfordshire Press

Hawes P and Perez B (1996) *The Gypsy and the State* (2nd edition), Bristol: Policy Press

Hester R (2004) *Services Provided to Gypsy Traveller Children*, Birmingham: NECF

Hetherington K (2000) *New Age Travellers: Vanloads of uproarious humanity*, London: Cassell

James Z (2005) 'Eliminating communities? Exploring the implications of policing methods used to manage New Travellers', *International Journal of the Sociology of Law*, 33, pp. 159–68

Jarman E and Jarman AOH (1998) *The Welsh Gypsies: Children of Abram Wood*, Cardiff: University of Wales Press

Joseph Rowntree Foundation (2007) *A Review of Research on the Links Between Education and Poverty: Findings 2122*, York: Joseph Rowntree Foundation

Kenrick D (1994) 'Irish Travellers: a unique phenomenon in Europe?', in McCann M, Siochain SO and Ruane J (eds) *Irish Travellers: Culture and ethnicity*, Belfast: Institute of Irish Studies, Queens University

Kenrick D and Clark C (1999) *Moving On: The Gypsies and Travellers of Britain*, Hatfield: University of Hertfordshire Press

Kiddle C (2000) 'Partnerships depend on power-sharing: an exploration of the relationships between Fairground and Gypsy Traveller parents and their children's teachers in England', *International Journal of Educational Research*, 33:3, pp. 265–274

Laming WH (2003) *The Victoria Climbié Inquiry: Report of an inquiry by Lord Laming*, London: DH

Lau A and Ridge M (2011) 'Addressing the impact of social exclusion on mental health in Gypsy, Roma, and Traveller communities', *Mental Health and Social Inclusion*, 15:3, pp. 129–137

Levinson M and Sparkes A (2003) *Gypsy Masculinity and the Home School Interface: Exploring contradictions and tensions*, London: Education Administrative Extracts

Liegeois J-P (1986) *Gypsies: An illustrated history*, London: Al Saqui Books

MacGabhann C (2011) *Voices Unheard: A study of Irish Travellers in prison*, London: The Irish Chaplaincy in Britain

Martin G (2002) 'New Age Travellers: uproarious or uprooted?', *Sociology*, 36:3, pp. 723–735

Mayall D (1995) *English Gypsies and State Policies*, Hatfield: University of Hertfordshire Press

McVeigh J (1997) 'Theorising sedentarism: the roots of antinomadism', in Acton T (ed) *Gypsy Politics and Traveller Identity*, Hatfield: University of Hertfordshire Press

Morran D (2001) 'A forgotten minority: workers' perceptions of Scottish Travelling People', *Probation Journal*, 48:1, pp. 26–33

Morran D (2002) 'Negotiating marginalised identities: social workers and settled Travelling People in Scotland', *International Social Work*, 45:3, pp. 337–51

Nexus (2006) *Moving Beyond Coping: An insight into the experiences and needs of Travellers in Tallaght in coping with suicide*, Tallaght: Travellers Youth Services

Niner P (2002) *The Provision and Condition of Local Authority Gypsy/ Traveller Sites in England*, London: Office of the Deputy Prime Minister (ODPM), accessed 24 February 2013, from www.communities.gov.uk/ publications/housing/203540

Ofsted (1999) *Raising the Attainment of Minority Ethnic Pupils*, London: Ofsted Publications Centre

O'Hanlon C and Holmes P (2004) *The Education of Gypsy and Traveller Children: Towards inclusion and educational achievement*, Stoke on Trent: Trentham Books

O'Higgins K (1993) 'Travelling children in substitute care', in O'Higgins K (ed) *Surviving Childhood Adversity*, Belfast: Institute of Irish Studies

Okely J (1983) *The Traveller Gypsy*, Cambridge: Cambridge University Press

Parker-Jenkins M and Hartas D (2002) 'Social inclusion: the case of Travellers' children', *Education* 3-13, 30:2, pp. 39–42

Parry G, van Cleemput P, Peters J, Moore J, Walters S, Thomas K and Cooper C (2004) *The Health Status of Gypsies and Travellers in England*, Sheffield: University of Sheffield

Pavee Point (2005) *Pavee Beoirs: Breaking the silence*. Traveller women and male domestic violence, Dublin: Pavee Point

Pemberton D (1999) 'Fostering in a minority community:Travellers in Ireland', in Greeff R (ed) *Fostering Kinship: An international perspective on kinship foster care*, Aldershot: Ashgate

Penketh L (2000) *Tackling Institutional Racism*, Bristol: Policy Press

Pizani Williams L (1996) *Gypsies and Travellers in the Criminal Justice System: The forgotten minority*, Cropwood Occasional Papers 23, Cambridge: University of Cambridge Institute of Criminology

Poole L and Adamson K (2008) *Report on the Situation of the Roma Community in Govanhill*, Glasgow: School of Social Sciences, University of West Scotland

Powell R (2007) 'Civilising offensives and ambivalence: the case of British Gypsies', *People, Place & Policy Online*, 1:3, pp. 112–123

Power C (2004) *Room to Roam: England's Irish Travellers*, London: The Community Fund

Power C (2007) *The Accommodation Situation of Showmen in the Northwest*, Bury, Lancs: The Showmen's Guild

Richardson J (2006) *The Gypsy Debate: Can discourse control?*, Thorverton: Imprint Academic

Richardson J, Allen D, Bloxsom J, Brown J, Cemlyn S, Greenfields, M and Lishman R (2010) *Somerset Gypsy and Traveller Accommodation Assessment*, Leicester: De Montfort University

Richardson J, Bloxsom J and Greenfields M (2007) *East Kent Sub-Regional Gypsy and Traveller Accommodation Assessment Report (2007–2012)*, Leicester: De Montfort University

Roberts A, Adkins J, Lewis H and Wilkinson C (2007) Community Practitioners' and Health Visitors' Assocation (CPHVA) *Annual Conference, Coronary Heart Disease and Mental Health in Gypsies and Travellers in Wrexham: Redressing the balance*, Torquay, 31 October–2 November 2007, accessed 12 March 2013, at www.amicus-cphva.org/pdf/B2.2%20Helen%20Lewis.pdf

Ryder A and Greenfields M (2010) *Roads to Success: Economic and social inclusion for Gypsies and Travellers*, London: Irish Traveller Movement in Britain

Saunders P, Clarke J, Kendall S, Lee A, Lee S and Matthews F (eds) (2000) *Gypsies and Travellers in their Own Words*, Leeds: Leeds Traveller Education Service

Scottish Parliament (2012) *Equal Opportunities Committee: 3rd Report, 2012 (Session 4) Gypsy/Travellers and Care Edinburgh: APS Group Scotland*, Edinburgh: Scottish Parliament

Shelter (2008) *Good Practice Guide: Working with housed Gypsies and Travellers*, London: Shelter

Smith R (2009) *Doing Social Work Research*, Maidenhead: Open University Press

Thompson N (2006) *Anti-Discriminatory Practice* (4th edition), Basingstoke: Macmillan

Tong D (ed) (1998) *Gypsies: An interdisciplinary reader*, Hatfield: University of Hertfordshire Press

van Cleemput P (2004) *The Health Status of Gypsies and Travellers in England. Report of Qualitative Findings*, Sheffield: University of Sheffield

Vanderbeck RM (2005) 'Anti-nomadism, institutions and the geographies of childhood', *Society and Space*, 23, pp. 71–94

Vonk M (2001) 'Cultural competence for transracial adoptive parents', *Social Work*, 46, pp. 246–255

Warrington J (2006) *Children's Voices: Changing futures*, Ipswich: Ormiston Children and Families Trust

Wired (2005) *Paul's Story*, Peterborough: Peterborough Nene Drug Intervention Programme, accessed 2 February 2013, at www.wiredinitiative.com/pdf/peterboroughstories/Paul.pdf

Worthington A (2005) *Battle of the Beanfield*, London: Enabler Publications